BODYTALK

BODYTALK

A World Guide to Gestures

DESMOND MORRIS

JONATHAN CAPE
LONDON

First published 1994

1 3 5 7 9 10 8 6 4 2

© Desmond Morris 1994

Desmond Morris has asserted his right
under the Copyright, Designs and Patents Act, 1988
to be identified as the author of this work

First published in the United Kingdom in 1994 by
Jonathan Cape
Random House, 20 Vauxhall Bridge Road, London SWIV 2SA

Random House Australia (Pty) Limited
20 Alfred Street, Milsons Point, Sydney,
New South Wales 2061, Australia

Random House New Zealand Limited
18 Poland Road, Glenfield,
Auckland10, New Zealand

Random House South Africa (Pty) Limited
PO Box 337, Bergvlei, South Africa

Random House UK Limited Reg. No. 954009

A CIP catalogue record for this book
is available from the British Library

ISBN 0-224-03969-5

Illustrations by Alan Austin

Typeset by SX Composing Ltd, Rayleigh, Essex

Printed in Great Britain by
Clays Ltd, St. Ives PLC

INTRODUCTION

Ever since human beings stood up on their hind legs and transformed their front feet into delicate hands, they have been gesticulating wildly. Their trudging, old front feet have become sensitive, new organs of communication. With considerable help from the most expressive faces in the animal kingdom, these amazing hands have developed a huge repertoire of complex body signals. It is this silent language that *Bodytalk* sets out to interpret.

As we move around the world we cannot help noticing that certain familiar gestures disappear and other strange ones take their place. What do they mean? It is all too easy to make mistakes, as every seasoned traveller will have discovered. What is polite in one region is obscene in another. What is friendly here, is hostile there. That is why a guide is needed.

Some gestures, intriguingly, do not suffer from these local variations. They appear to be universal and make us feel at least partially at home even when we are on the other side of the globe. A smile is a smile is a smile, the world over. A frown is a frown, a stare is a stare, and a shaken fist leaves no doubt about the mood of its owner. Some elements of body language, therefore, are more basic than others, but all benefit from study because even these global signals can vary in style and intensity. We all laugh, but in some places a loud laugh is considered rude. So even with our most basic signals it helps to understand the regional rules of conduct.

One of the problems that has to be faced when compiling a guide to gestures is what to leave out. Many gestures are so well known that it seems pointless to include them. Occasionally, unusual examples of common gestures have, however, been included. For instance, types of hand-holding and forehead kissing are shown because they appear in some countries in a way that might be misunderstood. But the ordinary hand-holding and forehead kissing that occur between, say, a parent and child are omitted because they are familiar to everyone.

Also omitted are the gestures that comprise the formal sign-language systems for which specific training is necessary. All the gestures shown in *Bodytalk* are 'informal' and are used, either consciously or unconsciously, by ordinary people as they go about their daily lives.

DESMOND MORRIS
Oxford, 1994

HOW TO USE THIS GUIDE

To make it easy to find your way around this guide, each gesture has been classified by its major body part. If a finger comes up to tap a nose, the gesture is called a Nose Tap and is found under N. If fingers are crossed and held aloft, the gesture is classified as Fingers Cross, and is found under F. For clarity, even a well-known gesture such as a wink is classified by its organ and is found under E for Eye Wink. So, to track down a gesture, all that is needed is to search alphabetically for the part of the body involved.

In every case there is a small sketch of the gesture. Alongside this there are four headings:

Meaning   –   Action   –   Background   –   Locality

The **Meaning** gives the basic message of the signal.

The **Action** describes the movements involved, as a supplement to the sketch.

The **Background** discusses anything known about the gesture, such as its origin, the context in which it is used and, where we have such information, its history.

The **Locality** tells where this gesture has been observed. In a few instances we know a great deal about the distribution of a gesture, but in many other cases we know only that it has been recorded in one particular country. So, if a gesture is classified as Locality: Holland, it does not necessarily mean that it is absent elsewhere. In future it is hoped to enlarge these records considerably, as we learn more and more about our fascinating human gestural language.

Gender Note: Anyone noticing that most of the sketches depict males might come to the conclusion that this shows an unfair gender bias. This is not the case. It is not this book that is sexist, it is the gestures themselves. For some reason, signalling by gesture is a predominantly masculine pursuit. In some countries it is so exclusively masculine that our female researcher had to withdraw before the local men would even discuss the subject.

ARM FLEX

Meaning: I am strong.

Action: The arm is bent to produce maximum bulging of the muscles.

Background: This stylized action of body-builders is used as joking social gesture when a male wishes to comment on his own strength.

Locality: Western world.

ARM GRASP

Meaning: Friendly greeting.

Action: While shaking hands, the gesturer's left hand grabs the arm of the companion.

Background: This reaching forward of the left arm is an incipient embrace, added to the formal hand-shake to give the routine greeting a stronger, more emotional impact. Occasionally, even this is not enough and the gesturer reaches around the back of the companion, offering a semi-embrace, while still shaking hands. Politicians sometimes deliberately employ these hand-shake 'intensifiers' to give the impression that they are exceptionally pleased to see someone.

Locality: Widespread in the Western world.

ARM RAISE (1)

Meaning: Request for attention.

Action: The arm is raised high in the air, palm showing, and held there until the gesture has been acknowledged.

Background: This is essentially a schoolroom gesture that has since spread into adult social life. It is employed at gatherings where someone wishes to speak and is also used when an informal vote is required.

Locality: Widespread.

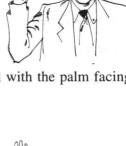

ARM RAISE (2)

Meaning: I swear.

Action: The right hand is raised to shoulder level and held still with the palm facing forward.

Locality: Western world.

ARM RAISE (3)

Meaning: Friendly greeting.

Action: The arm is raised with the palm showing and the fingers slightly spread.

Background: This is the greeting gesture used in milder situations than the full Hand Wave. Most commonly observed at fairly close quarters, as when acknowledging someone at a social gathering.

Locality: Widespread.

ARM RAISE (4)

Meaning: Hail!

Action: The arm is raised, palm showing, with the arm stiffly erect. The angle of the arm varies.

Background: This originated as a Roman salute and was revived by the German Nazis in the 1930s as a gesture of rigid loyalty. Still seen today in neo-Nazi political groups in Germany and elsewhere.

Locality: Originally Ancient Rome. Today in the Western world wherever extreme right-wing groups gather.

ARM SHAKE

Meaning: You are exaggerating.

Action: The arm, held low, brushes back and forth.

Background: As a signal of disbelief, the action says 'There are no flies on me!'

Locality: Arab cultures.

ARMPIT TICKLE

Meaning: Poor joke.

Action: The forefinger conspicuously tickles the gesturer's own armpit.

Background: This is a response to a joke that fails to create laughter. The message is 'I would have to tickle myself like this in order to make myself laugh at such a bad joke.'

Locality: Indonesia.

ARMPITS HOOK

Meaning: Pride.

Action: The thumbs are hooked into the armpits and the fingers are fanned out wide.

Background: This gesture is derived from the action of hooking the thumbs into the armholes of a waistcoat, or under the elastic of a pair of braces and stretching them forward. It is a smugly arrogant display of complete relaxation and says 'I am so pleased with myself that, while others must stay alert, I can afford to relax in this way, without a care in the world.' Today it is nearly always performed in jest.

Locality: Europe and North America.

ARMS AKIMBO (I)

Meaning: Keep away from me.

Action: The hands are placed on the hips so that the elbows protrude from the sides of the body.

Background: This is an unconscious action we perform when we feel anti-social in a social setting. It is observed when sportsmen have just lost a vital point, game or contest. It is as if they are automatically adopting an 'anti-embrace' posture without recognizing what they are doing. It also occurs at social gatherings when one person wishes to exclude another from a small group. In such cases, a single arm akimbo may be enough, pointing in the direction of the particular individual who is to be kept at a distance.

Locality: Worldwide.

ARMS AKIMBO (2)

Meaning: Anger.

Action: (As above)

Background: In some regions, the Arms Akimbo posture is adopted as a specific signal of seething rage. This is merely an exaggeration of its ordinary use, taking the 'upset' feelings of the usual akimbo posture and extending them into full outrage or anger.

Locality: Malaysia and the Philippines.

ARMS BEHIND

Meaning: I am at ease.

Action: The hands are clasped, one in the other, behind the back.

Background: When we feel anxious we tend to keep our hands in front of our bodies, like a defensive barrier. When we clamp them behind our backs it suggests that we are in precisely the opposite mood. In other words, we are saying 'I am so at ease that I do not need to protect myself and can display this posture, with the front of my body exposed.' In the army, the situation is slightly different, but the basic message is the same. There, it is the position soldiers must adopt when they are given the order to 'stand at ease'.

Locality: Widespread.

ARMS FOLD

Meaning: I feel defensive.

Action: The arms are folded across the chest.

Background: This is a common, unconscious resting posture frequently adopted by people who wish to set up a mild barrier between themselves and those in front of them. The arms act like a car-fender, protecting the front of the body from unwanted intrusions. Most people are unaware that they are displaying this 'barrier signal', but sometimes it can be used deliberately as a 'You shall not pass' sign – for example, by guards outside a doorway, trying to prevent someone from entering.

Locality: Worldwide.

ARMS RAISE (1)

Meaning: I surrender.

Action: The arms, slightly bent at the elbows, are raised with the palms facing forward.

Background: This is the 'Hands Up!' action performed to emphasize that no sudden, aggressive movement is about to be made. In violent situations it is employed seriously as a sign of capitulation, but it is also used jokingly in social contexts to say 'I give up!', when losing an argument.

Locality: Widespread.

ARMS RAISE (2)

Meaning: Prayer.

Action: The arms are raised high, usually with the palms facing upwards to the sky, and with the head tilted back.

Background: This is the most ancient posture of prayer. From the study of early works of art, we know that it was in existence long before the now familiar Palms Contact action appeared. It is used to ask for help from the deity, or to give thanks. In origin it is simply an embracing gesture in which the arms reach up to the deity in the heavens above. In its pre-religious form it can be seen in the behaviour of a small child who reaches up towards a standing parent, inviting a hug.

Locality: Widespread.

ARMS RAISE (3)

Meaning: Triumph.

Action: The arms are fully raised, usually without any elbow-bend. Often they are slightly splayed, creating a V shape.

Background: This is the posture of the victorious sportsman or politician. In origin it is a 'body enlargement' action, making the dominant figure seem taller.

Locality: Widespread.

ARMS REACH

Meaning: I offer you my embrace.

Action: The arms reach out as if to make an embrace, but the action cannot be completed because of the distance between the gesturer and his companions.

Background: This is the favoured gesture of public figures who have just completed a performance and wish to respond to the applause of their audience by hugging them all. Unable to do so, they simply make the 'intention movement' of embracing them.

Locality: Worldwide.

ARMS ROCK

Meaning: Baby.

Action: The arms mime the action of rocking a baby to sleep.

Background: This gesture is used in a variety of ways to refer to the presence of an infant. Most commonly it is employed to announce the presence of a baby that cannot for the moment be seen. It may also occasionally be used sarcastically to say to someone 'You are behaving like a baby.'

Locality: Widespread.

ARMS 'SHOVEL'

Meaning: You are talking nonsense.

Action: The arms mime the action of shovelling up manure and throwing it over the shoulder.

Background: This gesture is known as 'Throwing the bull' and is the gestural equivalent of the word 'bullshit'.

Locality: North America.

BEARD GROW

Meaning: How boring!

Action: The hand is placed under the chin and then drawn downwards as if stroking or measuring a long beard.

Background: This gesture is used in two contexts. If someone is making a long and boring speech, it is given to suggest 'One could grow a long beard while listening to this.' Or, if someone is telling an ancient and well-known joke, the gesture is made to say 'This joke is so old it has a beard.'

Locality: Holland, Germany, Austria and Italy.

BEARD STROKE (1)

Meaning: I am deep in thought.

Action: The hand is pulled pensively down through the beard a number of times, as if grooming it absent-mindedly.

Background: This is an unconscious action performed as a minor comfort device when wrestling with a difficult decision or a complex idea.

Locality: Common in Jewish communities but also observed worldwide.

BEARD STROKE (2)

Meaning: How boring!

Action: The beard (real or imaginary) is stroked with the fingers.

Background: This is a local version of the 'my beard is growing while you speak' gesture.

Locality: Austria.

BEARD WAG

Meaning: You are old.

Action: The fingers of one hand are held beneath the chin and wiggled.

Background: The fingers mime an old man's beard, implying great age, and possibly senility, in the other person.

Locality: Saudi Arabia.

BELLY 'CUT'

Meaning: I am hungry.

Action: The flat hand, with the palm down, cuts rhythmically sideways against the belly.

Background: The gesture implies that the pain of hunger is cutting into the belly.

Locality: Italy.

BELLY PAT

Meaning: I am full.

Action: The belly is patted gently with the hand.

Background: The gesture draws attention to the rounded shape of the full belly after a good meal.

Locality: Widespread.

BELLY PRESS

Meaning: Hunger.

Action: The fists are pressed hard against the belly, while the mouth is held open.

Background: The gesture mimes the agony of stomach pains caused by extreme hunger.

Locality: Latin America.

BELLY RUB (1)

Meaning: Hunger.

Action: The hand clasps the belly and makes a circular movement.

Background: The movement of the hand suggests the action employed to soothe the pain caused by an empty stomach.

Locality: Worldwide.

BELLY RUB (2)

Meaning: I enjoy your misfortune.

Action: The flat hand is rubbed up and down on the front of the belly.

Background: The gesture mimes the act of aching from too much belly-laughter.

Locality: Central Europe.

BELLY 'SLICE'

Meaning: None left!

Action: The flattened hand, palm up, slices across the belly from left to right.

Background: This gesture, associated with the phrases 'Ceinture' (Belt!) or 'Plus rein!' is easily confused with the Italian Belly 'Cut' signifying hunger.

Locality: France.

BODY KOWTOW (1)

Meaning: Subordination.

Action: The body kneels down and the head is then lowered until it touches the ground.

Background: This is an extreme form of body-lowering that is halfway between the kneel and full prostration. In earlier times it was given as a greeting to many dominant figures, but today it is largely confined to religious contexts, where the faithful are humbling themselves before the deity. It is still common in this role, as a posture of Muslim prayer.

Locality: Throughout the Muslim world.

BODY KOWTOW (2)

Meaning: Subordination.

Action: The body kneels down and the elbows are placed on the ground. The hands are brought together in front of the face.

Background: This modified version of the Kowtow is a combination of the full Kowtow and the Asiatic greeting in which the hands are placed together in front of the face. It was still being performed as an extreme form of submissive greeting in parts of the Orient at the end of the nineteenth century.

Locality: Laos.

BODY LEAN (1)

Meaning: I am paying attention.

Action: The body leans forward towards the companion.

Background: This is an unconscious body posture adopted by those who wish to indicate eager attentiveness. It is the posture of the subordinate facing his superior, the salesman talking to a buyer, and the doting lover. The more dominant figure is usually leaning back in a more relaxed position.

Locality: Worldwide.

BODY LEAN (2)

Meaning: I am about to leave.

Action: The seated body leans forward, with the hands gripping the chair.

Background: In this version, the figure is preparing to rise and the leaning posture is an 'intention movement' of departing.

Locality: Worldwide.

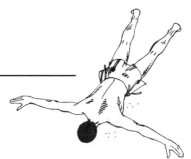

BODY PROSTRATE

Meaning: Submissive greeting.

Action: The body lies chest-down on the ground, with arms spread wide.

Background: In earlier centuries, all-powerful rulers were often greeted in this abject manner. Today's formal bow, curtsey and kneel are almost the only remnants of this once common form of human subordination. Like all displays by inferiors towards superiors, it involves body lowering that makes the displaying individual appear much smaller than normal. In this case, the height-reduction is taken to the ultimate extreme. Today it is hard to find any examples of full prostration in front of dominant human figures, but some cases of religious prostration do still occur in front of a sacred image or a deity.

Locality: Still occurs in some religious orders, and a few remote tribal cultures.

BREASTS CUP

Meaning: She is sexy.

Action: The hands make groping movements as if cupping large female breasts and fondling them.

Background: The gesture is used as a vulgar suggestion of what a man would like to do to a particular female.

Locality: European in origin but understood almost everywhere.

BREASTS OUTLINE

Meaning: She is sexy.

Action: The hands make a curving movement that outlines the shape of the female breasts.

Background: This gesture is used as a vulgar compliment by men discussing a well-rounded female.

Locality: European in origin but understood almost everywhere.

BREASTS THROW

Meaning: Big breasts.

Action: The gesturer mimes the act of flipping two pendulous breasts back over the shoulders.

Background: In some tribes the breasts of the women become so long and pendulous that they can be lifted up and back, over the shoulder, to feed a baby that is strapped to the back. This gesture mimes this action as a ribald comment on the impressive size of a woman's breasts.

Locality: South America.

BROW TAP

Meaning: Crazy!

Action: The thumb and forefinger tips are squeezed together as if holding some very small object. They are then tapped against the centre of the brow several times.

Background: The message of the gesture is that 'your brain is so small that I could hold it between my thumb and finger.' This is a local version of the more common Forehead Tap or Temple Tap, in which a forefinger taps the side of the forehead or the temple region.

Locality: Italy, especially Naples.

BROW TOUCH

Meaning: I cannot do it.

Action: The tip of the forefinger touches the centre of the brow-ridge, between the eyebrows.

Background: The gesture appears to mimic shooting oneself between the eyes. It is a signal of shame, the essential message being 'I am ashamed that I cannot do this thing.'

Locality: Saudi Arabia.

BUTTOCK PAT

Meaning: Encouragement.

Action: The male companion's buttock is given a single, friendly pat.

Background: This is a sportsman's gesture, which takes the place of the more usual encouraging shoulder pat. Its most common context is in American Football, where it may have originated due to the heavy padding of the shoulders that made the shoulder pat inappropriate there. From this beginning it has now spread to other sports. It remains rare in non-sporting, social situations because of the possible confusion with other buttock contacts that carry a sexual implication.

Locality: Primarily North American, but now also in Europe.

BUTTOCK SLAP

Meaning: Insult.

Action: The right buttock is thrust out and the right hand moves as if to slap it. In a variation of this, the slap is carried through.

Background: This insult can carry either of two messages: 'You should be spanked' and 'Kiss my arse'.

Locality: Germany, Austria, Eastern Europe and the Middle East.

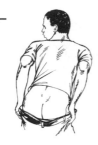

BUTTOCKS EXPOSE

Meaning: Kiss my arse.

Action: The clothing is briefly removed to display the naked buttocks. The effect is increased by bending forward.

Background: This form of insult is illegal in some regions, but is merely treated as a rude joke in others. The illegality is often judged on the basis of whether the 'organs of procreation' are made visible by the action, in addition to the buttocks. In modern times the intention of the display is to say to the victim either: 'I defecate on you' or 'Kiss my arse.' The latter message is an ancient one and there is more to it than mere humiliation. The human species is the only primate to possess a pair of rounded buttocks. In earlier centuries it was believed that this made the Devil intensely envious. Lacking buttocks himself, Satan was outraged by any reminder of this fact. To show him your naked buttocks was therefore an excellent protection against the Evil Eye. And since the Devil, in place of buttocks, carried on his rump a second face, it became a familiar taunt to shout out 'Kiss my arse' when the display was aimed at human companions. This implied that the victims of the insult were no better than loathsome Satanists. Today all these details are forgotten, but the insult lives on. In the 1960s this action became a popular taunt among American female college students. Usually performed from the safety of an upstairs window, it became known as 'mooning'.

Locality: Europe and North America.

BUTTOCKS SLAP

Meaning: Obscene insult.

Action: The body bends over to show the buttocks and the hand is brought round to slap them centrally.

Background: This more extreme form of slap is an exaggerated version of the 'Kiss my arse' display.

Locality: Eastern Europe and the Middle East.

BUTTOCKS THRUST

Meaning: Obscene disdain.

Action: The buttocks are thrust backwards towards the insulted person.

Background: This simple gesture is essentially an excretory insult, with the message 'I defecate on you'.

Locality: Southern Italy.

CHEEK BRUSH (1)

Meaning: How boring.

Action: The backs of the fingers are brushed back and forth against the cheek, as if testing the growth of beard there.

Background: The French word for beard – 'barbe' – also means boring. This relates back to a time when there was a saying to the effect that 'I could grow a beard while listening to your interminable droning.'

Locality: France.

CHEEK BRUSH (2)

Meaning: I am not sure.

Action: (As above)

Background: The unconscious, thoughtful rubbing of the cheek that occurs when someone is confused has been stylized as a deliberate signal, saying 'I don't follow you', 'I have my doubts about what you are saying', or 'I really don't understand you.'

Locality: United States.

CHEEK CREASE

Meaning: Sarcasm.

Action: One mouth corner is drawn back strongly, so that it forms a crease in the cheek.

Background: This is a deliberately distorted version of the smile. As a 'deformed compliment' it transmits a signal that is sardonic or sarcastic.

Locality: Widespread in the Western world.

CHEEK 'CUT'

Meaning: He is tough.

Action: The thumb mimes the action of cutting the cheek with a knife or razor. The nail of the thumb is drawn forcibly down the cheek, from ear to mouth.

Background: This is a gesture that suggests someone is a 'scar-carrying member of the gang'. He is therefore tough and a serious threat.

Locality: Italy, especially in the Neapolitan region.

CHEEK DEFLATE

Meaning: Nonsense!

Action: The cheeks are puffed up and then deflated by a blow from the bunched fingertips of the right hand.

Background: The symbolism implies that someone is full of hot air and needs deflating because he is speaking nonsense.

Locality: France and the Middle East.

CHEEK DOWN-RUB

Meaning: I swear!

Action: The palm strikes the cheek and is then rubbed downwards.

Background: The action is used to reinforce the swearing of an oath.

Locality: Saudi Arabia.

CHEEK KISS

Meaning: Friendly greeting.

Action: Mutual cheek-kissing is performed first on one cheek and then the other.

Background: The cheek kiss is favoured as a greeting today for several reasons: (1) Because the two people involved perform identical actions, it signals equal status; (2) It avoids the sexual implications of the mouth to mouth kiss; (3) It demonstrates that two people are intimate friends and not merely acquaintances; (4) It permits an intimate act without the need for the lips to make actual skin contact. The lips can kiss close to the cheek instead of resting on it. In this way, female make-up is not damaged. The popularity of the Cheek Kiss varies, not so much from region to region, as social group to social group. It is most commonly observed among the upper classes and in the theatrical world. The middle classes are now copying it more than in the past.

Locality: Western world.

CHEEK 'LATHER'

Meaning: You are trying to fool me.

Action: The right forefinger makes a circular motion on the cheek, as if lathering the skin before shaving.

Background: The essential message of this gesture is 'I know what you are up to – you are trying to take me in – but you won't succeed.'

Locality: France.

CHEEK PINCH (1)

Meaning: Excellent.

Action: The cheek is pinched between the gesturer's thumb and forefinger.

Background: The action mimics the moment when a parent praises an infant by gently pinching its cheek. Now, the act of praise is re-enacted as a comment on the excellence of some object, event or person.

Locality: Italy.

CHEEK PINCH (2)

Meaning: Playful affection.

Action: The flesh of a companion's cheek is gently pinched between thumb and forefinger.

Background: When performed between adults this gesture mimics the action of a parent with an infant. In aggressive encounters it has a special, threatening meaning: 'you are a child in my hands'.

Locality: Most commonly seen in the Mediterranean region.

CHEEK SCRAPE

Meaning: Thief.

Action: The fingertips of a slightly cupped hand scrape gently down one cheek, several times.

Background: This 'clawing' movement suggests the thieving hand feeling gently for something to steal.

Locality: South America.

CHEEK SCREW (1)

Meaning: Superb!

Action: The forefinger, or a combination of the thumb-and-forefinger, are screwed into the centre of the cheek.

Background: This gesture usually refers to food, but may also be employed as a compliment to a beautiful girl. When applied to food, it is often accompanied by the phrase 'al dente', meaning tasty or, literally, 'on the tooth'. It is applied especially to pasta which has been cooked to precisely the right degree.

Locality: Italy.

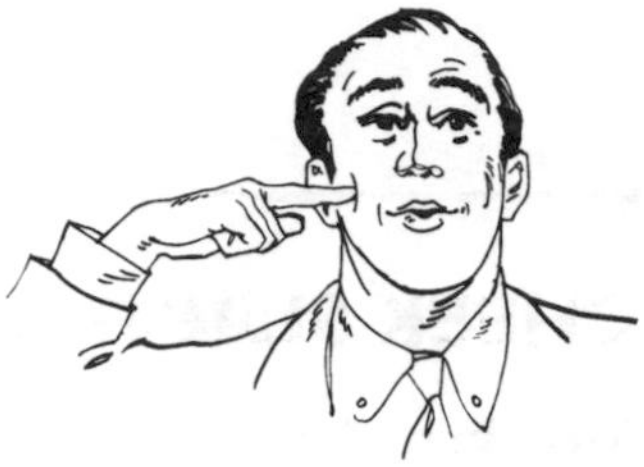

CHEEK SCREW (2)

Meaning: She is beautiful.

Action: The stiff forefinger is screwed into the cheek.

Background: The gesture indents a dimple, a traditional sign of feminine beauty.

Locality: Italy and Libya.

CHEEK SCREW (3)

Meaning: He is effeminate.

Action: (As above)

Background: When the action is directed at a woman it is a compliment, but when it is made towards a man it is employed as an insult, implying dimpled effeminacy.

Locality: Southern Spain.

CHEEK SCREW (4)

Meaning: You are crazy!

Action: (As above)

Background: In some regions, the police prosecute people who make rude gestures at them. German police react in this way to the well-known Temple Screw gesture, meaning 'crazy'. As a defence against this, some Germans use the Cheek Screw as a covert form of Temple Screw. The movement made by the finger is the same, but by pressing it against the cheek instead of the temple, the gesturer can claim he was reacting to a painful tooth.

Locality: Germany.

CHEEK SLAP

Meaning: Shocked surprise.

Action: Lightly slapping your own cheek.

Background: It mimics the act of being slapped on the cheek by someone else. Its message is that 'I am as shocked as if someone else were to slap me like this.' It usually occurs at the moment when the gesturer suddenly realizes that he or she has done something stupid, for which they deserve to be slapped.

Locality: Widespread.

CHEEK SUPPORT (I)

Meaning: Sissy!

Action: The head is tilted sideways and the cheek is rested on the palm of the hand in a deliberate, exaggerated action.

Background: This teasing gesture, which signals that someone is behaving like a baby, mimes the infantile act of cuddling up to mother and pressing the cheek comfortingly against her body.

Locality: Spain.

CHEEK SUPPORT (2)

Meaning: I am tired.

Action: (As above)

Background: The gesture mimes the action of laying the head on a pillow. It is easy to confuse this version of the gesture with the previous one, but in this case the expression on the face usually shows more exhaustion.

Locality: Common in Europe and widespread elsewhere.

CHEEKS INFLATE

Meaning: Fat.

Action: The cheeks are filled with air and held puffed out for a moment. The hands may support the action by describing a large, round shape.

Locality: Widespread.

CHEEKS STROKE (1)

Meaning: Thin and ill.

Action: The thumb and forefinger are drawn down the cheeks.

Background: The gesture suggests that someone's cheeks are hollow and sunken through illness or because they are unnaturally thin.

Locality: Widespread throughout Europe. Most common in Holland, Germany and Italy.

CHEEKS STROKE (2)

Meaning: Beautiful.

Action: As above, but with a more gentle, caressing movement. Sometimes the thumb and forefinger tips meet at the bottom of the chin.

Background: This gesture is known from as early as 1832 when it was described as indicating the 'Greek ideal' of beauty. The ancient Greeks preferred a woman's face to be egg-shaped and the Cheeks Stroke gesture was said to delineate this contour.

Locality: Today it is still common in northern Greece, and is also observed occasionally in other parts of that country and in the Mediterranean zone generally.

CHEST BEAT

Meaning: I am strong.

Action: The chest is struck several times with one or both fists.

Background: Because female breasts make this gesture difficult, it is favoured by males as a way of emphasizing their masculinity.

Locality: Widespread.

CHEST CROSS

Meaning: I swear.

Action: The hands are crossed and placed flat on the chest.

Background: By folding over one another, the hands make the sacred sign of the cross. Used in some regions when swearing an oath, this gesture is also employed during prayer and is frequently seen as the posture of death when a corpse has been formally laid out.

Locality: Most commonly observed in Italy.

CHEST HOLD

Meaning: Me?

Action: The palm of one hand is placed on the chest.

Background: This gesture is most frequently used when a companion is accused of something and replies 'Who, me?' As he does so, he places a hand, or hands, on his chest and holds it there. In the western world, the chest is often used to indicate 'self', as if the personality of the gesturer resides there, rather than in some other part of the body. The origin of this association can be traced back to the time when it was believed that the soul is embodied in the breath – 'the breath of life'. Since the lungs are in the chest, it follows that this must be the seat of the soul.

Locality: Widespread, especially in the Western world.

24

CHEST POINT

Meaning: Me?

Action: The forefinger is pointed at the chest and remains touching it for a few moments.

Background: As in the previous gesture, the chest is being used as the location of the 'self'. Here, however, there is a slightly different flavour to the message. With the previous gesture there is usually an element of denial: 'It's not me!' but with the Chest Point there is more of a simple questioning, such as: 'Is it me you want?' In addition it can also be used as a simple statement of 'self' during conversation.

Locality: Widespread.

CHEST PRESS

Meaning: He is a miser.

Action: The clenched fist or fists are pressed against the chest.

Background: The gesture implies that someone clasps everything to their bosom and keeps everything for themselves.

Locality: Italy and South America.

CHEST STROKE

Meaning: He is a miser.

Action: The first two fingers, with the others closed, are moved up and down the chest.

Background: Because touching the chest is the common way of signalling 'me', this gesture indicates someone who thinks only of himself.

Locality: Italy.

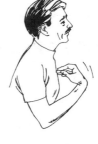

CHEST TAP (I)

Meaning: Me!

Action: The bunched fingertips of one or both hands are tapped against the chest.

Background: The chest is being used as the site of the 'self'. The gesture is usually made as a way of emphasizing 'me' during a conversation.

Locality: Worldwide.

CHEST TAP (2)

Meaning: I am bored.

Action: The hand, fingers pointing down, is tapped slowly and rhythmically against the chest.

Background: The gesture mimics the reaction to indigestion, implying that the companion is proving to be an 'indigestible' speaker.

Locality: Italy.

CHEST THUMP

Meaning: Woman.

Action: The (male) chest is thumped once with both fists.

Background: The fists symbolize the female breasts.

Locality: Greece.

CHEST-MOUTH-FOREHEAD SALAAM

Meaning: Formal greeting or farewell.

Action: The hand touches the chest, then the lips, then the centre of the forehead. The action ends with a forward flourish of the hand and is often accompanied by a bow of the head.

Background: This is the full version of the salaam, including all three elements. Its message is 'I give you my heart, my soul and my head.' It is used mostly on formal occasions. For everyday use, abbreviated forms are employed in which certain elements are omitted. The most common abbreviations are: Forehead only; Forehead and Chest; Mouth only; Mouth and Forehead.

Locality: Arab countries.

CHIN CHUCK

Meaning: Keep cheerful.

Action: The forefinger is gently pushed under the jawline of the companion, with a very slight upward pressure.

Background: This gesture derives from the fact that during moments of misery and depression the chin droops, and in more cheerful moments it is held high. By gently raising it a little, the gesturer attempts to cheer up the companion, often with the added phrase 'keep your chin up'.

Locality: Widespread.

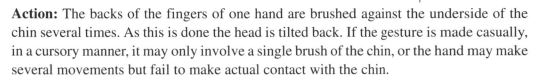

CHIN FLICK (1)

Meaning: No!

Action: The backs of the fingers of one hand are brushed against the underside of the chin several times. As this is done the head is tilted back. If the gesture is made casually, in a cursory manner, it may only involve a single brush of the chin, or the hand may make several movements but fail to make actual contact with the chin.

Background: This is a modified version of the Greek Head Tilt, the movement of the hand delineating and therefore amplifying the backward tilt.

Locality: Italy, from Naples to the south, including Sicily and Sardinia. Also common in Malta and Corfu.

CHIN FLICK (2)

Meaning: Aggressive disinterest.

Action: (As above)

Background: In this version of the gesture there is a different origin. Here it is a symbolic 'beard flip', the gesturer brushing his imaginary beard forward towards the onlooker. This origin is supported by the fact that in France the action is known as 'La Barbe', 'The Beard'. The symbolism of the gesture is that 'I show you my masculine maturity' and this is meant to carry a threatening message, such as 'Clear off', 'Shut up', 'I couldn't care less', 'I don't give a damn', 'I have had enough of you', or 'You bore me'.

Locality: Belgium, France, northern Italy, Tunisia and Yugoslavia.

CHIN FLICK (3)

Meaning: Disbelief.

Action: (As above)

Background: A minor meaning for this gesture, found in certain parts of Europe, is one of mildly aggressive disbelief, carrying a message such as 'I don't believe you', 'You are lying' or 'There's no truth in it'.

Locality: Greece and northern France.

CHIN FLICK (4)

Meaning: I have nothing.

Action: (As above)

Background: Another small variation in meaning for this multi-message gesture. Although the Chin Flick gesture carries a variety of local meanings, they all have one thing in common – they carry a negative signal of some kind.

Locality: Greece.

CHIN FLICK (5)

Meaning: I don't know.

Action: (As above)

Background: As a negative signal, this is a variant of the 'No' Chin Flick.

Locality: Portugal.

CHIN GRASP (1)

Meaning: Wisdom.

Action: The chin is grasped between the horizontal thumb and forefinger.

Background: In this gesture the hand takes hold of an imaginary (or real) beard. The implication is that anyone who wears a beard must be mature and wise. Clearly a gesture from a male-dominated society.

Locality: Saudi Arabia.

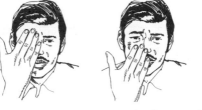

CHIN GRASP (2)

Meaning: I promise.

Action: The palm of the right hand is rubbed down the face until it reaches the chin, which is then grasped between the tips of the fingers and the thumb.

Background: It is easy to confuse the final stage of this gesture with the previous (and the following) gesture, especially as they are all observed in the same locality.

Locality: Saudi Arabia.

CHIN HOLD

Meaning: Please help me.

Action: The chin is grasped with thc tips of the fingers of the right hand.

Locality: Saudi Arabia.

CHIN HOOK (I)

Meaning: Defiant insult – Yah!

Action: The thumb is hooked under the chin and flicked vigorously forward several times.

Background: This is closely related to the Chin Flick. It is used mostly by children. Once a popular taunt, it is less common today.

Locality: Europe, especially Holland and France.

CHIN HOOK (2)

Meaning: It is over.

Action: (As above)

Background: This is another modified version of the Chin Flick, with a local meaning. It is used to signal that something no longer exists or that something has died. Like all the Chin Flick gestures, the Chin Hook gestures carry a negative message.

Locality: Portugal.

CHIN JUT

Meaning: Threat.

Action: The chin is thrust towards the companion.

Background: The human chin is unique among primates. The outward protuberance of bone at the front of the lower jaw is not found in other species. It is much more pronounced in human males than in females and appears to have evolved as a supporting structure for the adult male beard. In the primeval, unshaved condition, the jutting of the chin as an aggressive 'intention movement' of a forward attack would have the effect of thrusting the beard towards the enemy. Even today, with clean-shaven males, a slight thrusting movement of the chin towards a companion still automatically registers as a hostile act. The same jutting action can be observed in women, but their smaller chin makes the gesture inevitably less impressive.

Locality: Worldwide.

CHIN KNUCKLE

Meaning: It is your own fault.

Action: The knuckles of one hand are placed under the chin and rubbed forwards.

Locality: Indonesia.

CHIN LIFT

Meaning: I am above such things!

Action: The chin is lifted high. While this is done, the eyes are either closed or 'look down the nose' at the companion.

Background: This is the 'snobbery posture'. Today it is rarely performed seriously, because in an egalitarian social climate, such blatant displays of high status are unacceptable. But it is still frequently performed in jest, as a sign of mock outrage in response to a joke insult. (It has also been described as a 'nose in the air' or Nose Up gesture.)

Locality: Worldwide.

CHIN POINT

Meaning: Over there.

Action: The chin is thrust briefly in a particular direction.

Background: This is the casual pointing gesture of someone whose hands are busy. It is usually confined to close quarters, when a question is being asked about where some object or person is located. It can also be observed in cultures where finger-pointing is considered to be rude. In such cases it is an alternative to the more conspicuous Lips Point gesture.

Locality: Widespread.

CHIN RUB

Meaning: I do not believe you.

Action: The fingers rub the chin.

Background: Unconscious face-touching gestures indicate disbelief in what is being said by the companion. When listeners resort to the Chin Rub gesture, they are saying, in effect, 'I want to tell you that I do not believe you, but politeness prevents me from doing so. Because of this I am in a state of conflict. To ease that conflict I must perform a minor act of self-comfort. Self-contact gives me that sense of self-comfort.' This complex message is often overlooked by the speaker, who is preoccupied with his ideas, and he misses the clue that would tell him he is failing to convince his companion.

Locality: Worldwide.

CHIN SCRATCH

Meaning: Insult.

Action: The chin is scratched downwards, just below the mouth, with the forefinger and middle finger.

Background: This appears to have originated as a deliberate, stylized version of the unconscious Chin Rub, with the 'I don't believe you' meaning becoming an insult in the form of 'you are talking rubbish'.

Locality: Germany and Austria.

CHIN STROKE (1)

Meaning: I am thinking.

Action: The hand gently strokes the chin.

Background: This is the pensive Beard Stroke gesture performed on a beardless chin. This unconscious action is so basic that it is still performed even in the absence of the male beard. Because of its link with the beard, it is much more common in clean-shaven males than in females.

Locality: Worldwide.

CHIN STROKE (2)

Meaning: Respect.

Action: The fingers stroke the chin downwards as if caressing a beard.

Background: The symbolism of the gesture equates the male beard with maturity and wisdom. This is a variation of the Chin Grasp (1) gesture.

Locality: Saudi Arabia.

CHIN STROKE (3)

Meaning: It's in the bag!

Action: The chin is stroked by the thumb and forefinger.

Locality: Brazil.

CHIN SUPPORT

Meaning: Boredom.

Action: The chin is supported by the hand.

Background: This gesture is employed by someone trying to focus their attention on a speaker. It may make the gesturer look thoughtful, but its underlying message is that 'it is hard to concentrate' and implies a degree of boredom with what is being said.

Locality: Worldwide.

CHIN TAP

Meaning: I am fed up to here.

Action: The chin is tapped several times from below.

Background: The message is that the gesturer has had enough. Originally it signified someone who was full of food. It is now more commonly used to indicate that someone is emotionally fed up rather than well fed.

Locality: Western Europe and the Americas.

CHIN THUMB (1)

Meaning: I don't have any.

Action: The thumb rests on the chin while the fanned out fingers waggle from side to side.

Background: This appears to be a modified, milder version of the well-known Nose Thumb. The basic message is 'Go away, don't bother me any more.' It is a gesture often seen in the public market place.

Locality: Colombia.

CHIN THUMB (2)

Meaning: I have been stood up.

Action: (As above)

Background: In a social context, this gesture takes on the meaning of 'Disappointment' instead of 'Denial'. The 'I don't have any' message of the market place becomes transformed into 'I don't have any luck'.

Locality: Colombia.

CHIN TOUCH

Meaning: He is effeminate.

Action: The tip of the forefinger is placed under the chin, while the face adopts a softly smiling expression.

Background: This gesture is used by males as a mock female action to insult the masculinity of other men. The message is 'he is a pansy'.

Locality: Common in South America, but also observed elsewhere.

CHIN WITHDRAW

Meaning: Fear.

Action: The chin is retracted.

Background: This is the antithesis of the aggressive Chin Jut gesture. As an automatic response it is part of a protective action when someone is physically threatened. But it is also used as a deliberate gesture when the performer wishes to signal that something is scary or frightening.

Locality: Worldwide.

CLOTHING PULL (1)

Meaning: This is repetitious.

Action: The listener grasps a section of their clothing, bunching it in the hand, and then tugs at it, pulling it forward or to one side.

Background: This is essentially a boredom signal with the hand mimicking what the listener wants to happen, namely someone dragging them away from the boring speaker.

Locality: South America.

CLOTHING PULL (2)

Meaning: She is pregnant.

Action: The clothing is pulled forward to suggest a pregnant shape.

Background: This is a way of signalling that someone is pregnant, even if the •woman in question has, as yet, shown no outward signs of being so. In effect, the gesture says 'this is what is to come'. It may be used as a simple announcement or as malicious gossip.

Locality: Southern Italy.

CLOTHING SHAKE (1)

Meaning: I have finished with him.

Action: The hand shakes imaginary dust from the clothing.

Background: The symbolic message of this action is that 'I am cleansing myself of this relationship'. This is amplified by spitting on the ground - an additional 'cleansing of the throat'. The gesture is usually performed only by women.

Locality: Gypsy communities.

CLOTHING SHAKE (2)

Meaning: I had nothing to do with it.

Action: A speaker shakes his clothing vigorously with both hands.

Background: This gesture accompanies the bringing of bad news, to ensure that the messenger is not blamed for the message.

Locality: Arab countries.

COLLAR HOLD

Meaning: We are being deceived.

Action: The hand is brought up to lift the gesturer's own collar.

Background: This is an old gesture, known from as long ago as the 18th century, that is made when it is thought that a companion is cheating in some way. Usually, the fingers are inserted between the collar and the neck and the cloth is then pulled out slightly, away from the neck. In some cases, when the hand is inserted, the neck is stroked with the back of the hand. If the gesturer wishes to conceal the gesture from the 'cheat', it may be performed covertly by simply bringing the hand up close to the collar, as if about to carry out the full action. In contexts where companions are beginning to suspect that they are being deceived, this 'intention movement' of making the gesture will be sufficient to transmit the message between them, without alerting the 'cheat' to the fact that he has been found out.

Locality: Italy, especially the Neapolitan region.

COLLAR PULL

Meaning: I have been found out.

Action: The forefinger tugs at the collar to loosen it.

Background: This is the unconsciously performed gesture on which the phrase 'feeling hot under the collar' is based. When someone is lying and fears they have been caught out, there is a slight rise in their body temperature. This leads to some skin discomfort and the hand automatically moves towards the collar to loosen it.

Locality: Widespread.

CROTCH SCRATCH

Meaning: Sexual insult.

Action: The hand reaches down and conspicuously scratches the male genitals.

Background: This male gesture is employed as a gross insult, usually at a considerable distance from the victim. For example, a bullfighter who is being booed by a dissatisfied crowd may respond in this manner as a retaliation. In the southern states of the USA, policemen were photographed performing this action towards freedom marchers. The gesture has two insulting elements. In the first, the gesturer is saying: 'You are such scum that I am even prepared to perform this intimate act of scratching my genitals in front of you without the slightest embarrassment'. The second element is the common phallic insult of 'Up yours!', the scratching movement drawing attention to the relevant part of the gesturer's anatomy.

Locality: Central America, especially Mexico, but also observed in the southern states of North America.

CROWN TOUCH

Meaning: I swear.

Action: The flat palm is placed on the crown of the head.

Background: The gesturer performs on himself the 'laying on of hands'.

Locality: Middle East.

CUFF HOLD

Meaning: Apprehension.

Action: The hand adjusts the shirt cuff.

Background: This is an unconscious action that reveals a slight nervousness. It is most commonly observed on formal occasions when a visiting dignitary must cross an open space before being greeted by his hosts. Feeling apprehensive, he reaches across and grasps or fiddles with the cuff (or wristwatch, or cufflink) on the other arm. In doing so, he automatically creates a defensive 'barrier' across the front of his body. This 'body cross' shield gives him an increased sense of security. A female equivalent would be the slight adjustment of the position of the handbag on the opposite arm. Actions of this kind are known as 'barrier signals'.

Locality: Western world.

EAR CIRCLE

Meaning: Be good, or I will punish you!

Action: The stiff forefinger makes a circling motion around the ear.

Background: This is a stylized threat by a parent towards a child who is behaving badly, indicating that there may be punishment later if the misbehaviour does not cease. This is a local variant of the more common Ear Grasp gesture in which the parent grabs his or her own ear, as a threat of what may be done to the child later. Tweaking the ear of a child or tugging it along by its ear is a form of parental punishment observed in many cultures.

Locality: Saudi Arabia.

EAR CUP

Meaning: Speak up!

Action: The hand is cupped to the ear.

Background: This action, employed in a prolonged form when a listener is straining to catch someone's words, aids their hearing by artificially enlarging the 'dish' of the ear-pinna. In addition to this primary function, the action is used as a deliberate gesture to signal that someone is speaking too softly. When it is employed in this way, the hand is only held to the ear momentarily.

Locality: Worldwide.

EAR FLICK (1)

Meaning: I dislike him.

Action: The ear is flicked while speaking to someone.

Background: This gesture is saying 'That person is so unpleasant that someone should punish him' and refers to the widespread parental punishment of taking hold of a child by the ear.

Locality: Russia.

EAR FLICK (2)

Meaning: He is effeminate.

Action: The ear is flicked from behind several times.

Background: This gesture is employed as an insult by one man to another, carrying the message 'you are such a pansy that you should be wearing earrings.' The action of the forefinger, as it flicks the ear, is intended as a mime of drawing attention to a female earring. The Ear Tug gesture carries a similar message.

Locality: Italy.

EAR FLIP

Meaning: Do not argue with me.

Action: A forefinger is hooked around the back of the ear and then flipped forward.

Background: This action is a threat that the gesturer will 'take the victim by the ear' if they do not cease their opposition.

Locality: Saudi Arabia.

EAR GRASP

Meaning: Warning.

Action: The ear is held tightly between forefinger and thumb.

Background: This gesture is a mimed act of grabbing a child by the ear as an act of punishment. The adult threatens the child by grasping his own ear, saying, in effect 'This is what I will do to you if you don't behave yourself'.

Locality: Common in Greece and Turkey but not unknown elsewhere.

EAR HOLD (I)

Meaning: Disbelief.

Action: The ear is held between forefinger and thumb.

Background: The origin of this gesture is simply 'I do not believe my ears!'

Locality: Parts of northern Europe, especially Scotland.

EAR HOLD (2)

Meaning: Sponger.

Action: The earlobe is held between thumb and forefinger.

Background: This gesture is made by a man in a bar about a companion of his who has failed to buy his round of drinks. He says, in effect, 'He left me hanging with the bill, hanging like an earlobe.'

Locality: Spain and the Canary Islands. Also reported from England, where it is known in parts of London, the verbal description of a sponger or cadger there being: 'He is on the ear'ole'.

EAR NIBBLE

Meaning: I love you.

Action: The companion's ear is nibbled gently. The nibbling is usually interspersed with sucking, nuzzling and licking actions.

Background: This is part of sexual foreplay. During arousal, the lobes of the ear become engorged with blood and highly sensitive to touch. Since they have no other function, it would appear that these fleshy lobes, unique to the human species, have evolved specifically as an additional erogenous zone.

Locality: Worldwide.

EAR PULL

Meaning: Please talk straight!

Action: The arm is brought up over the head so that the hand can pull the ear on the opposite side.

Background: This is a deliberately distorted gesture that symbolizes the convoluted comments being made by a companion. It requests a simple, uncomplicated, straight-forward statement.

Locality: Jewish communities.

EAR RUB (1)

Meaning: I don't wish to hear this.

Action: The ear is rubbed between thumb and forefinger.

Background: This is an unconscious gesture used by adults when they wish to blot out the words they are hearing. It is a disguised version of the blatant 'cover-the-ears' reaction to an unpleasant noise. There is a secret wish to block the ears, but politeness prevents this. It does not, however, stop the hand from reaching up towards the ear. Once there it has to do something, and rubs the ear as a token reaction. This gesture should not be confused with the various deliberate forms of ear contact.

Locality: Worldwide.

EAR RUB (2)

Meaning: Do you want me to answer the question for you?

Action: The earlobe is rubbed between the forefinger and thumb.

Background: Unlike the previous gesture, this is a deliberate action.

Locality: Saudi Arabia.

EAR SCRATCH

Meaning: Confusion.

Action: The bent forefinger scratches behind the ear.

Background: This is an unconscious action – a small grooming movement associated with puzzlement. It indicates either that the gesturer is perplexed or, more specifically, that he does not believe what he is hearing.

Locality: Worldwide.

EAR TAP

Meaning: Protection.

Action: The ear is tapped with the fingers.

Background: This gesture is similar to 'touching wood' as a protective device. In earlier days, many people used to 'touch metal' rather than 'touch wood', because metal was then so precious that it was thought to have magical powers. The most common site for metal on the human body was the ear, where large ornamental earrings were commonly worn.

Locality: Turkey.

EAR THUMB (1)

Meaning: Joking insult.

Action: The thumb is placed in the ear and the fingers are fanned out sideways and waggled at the companion.

Background: This is a mild version of the Ears Thumb gesture which uses both hands at once. It is a playful insult employed mostly by children, saying 'you have a big ear like a silly donkey'. In other words, 'you are stupid'.

Locality: Widespread.

EAR THUMB (2)

Meaning: I have no money.

Action: (As above)

Background: The origin of this gesture is obscure. It may be a local variation of the Ear Thumb insult, but turned upon the gesturer himself. He is saying, in effect, 'I am a stupid donkey to have run out of money.'

Locality: Portugal.

EAR TOUCH

Meaning: Informer.

Action: The ear is touched with the fingers.

Background: Here the gesture means that someone is 'all ears' and is listening in to the conversation in order to pass on information to the authorities or to a rival.

Locality: Observed on the small island of Malta in the Mediterranean, and also reported from Staffordshire in England, where it is known as 'ear'oling'. It may have been taken to Malta by British troops.

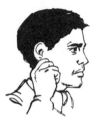

EAR TUG

Meaning: Effeminate.

Action: The earlobe is held between thumb and forefinger and tugged.

Background: This gesture is used as a sexist insult by one man to another, suggesting that the victim of the insult 'should be wearing earrings like a woman'. Some observers have reported that, in certain instances, it has a stronger meaning, namely 'you are so effeminate that you are impotent.' It has sometimes been confused with other ear contact gestures, with unfortunate results.

Locality: This gesture is confined almost entirely to Italy, including Sicily and Sardinia.

EAR WIGGLE

Meaning: Excellent!

Action: The earlobe is held gently between the forefinger and thumb and then waggled slightly.

Background: Men use this to indicate a delicious woman or delicious food. At the end of a good meal, a guest may compliment the hostess by kissing the side of his forefinger and then performing the Ear Wiggle. This gesture may be accompanied by the phrase 'behind the ear', but its origin is not clear. It has sometimes been confused with the Italian Ear Flick or Ear Hold gestures, meaning 'effeminate', with disastrous results.

Locality: Portugal and Brazil. It has also been observed on the campus of the University of California at Berkeley as a 'pleasure signal', but it is not clear how it arrived there.

EARS BLOCK

Meaning: Stop that noise!

Action: The tips of the forefingers are pushed into the ears.

Background: In its primary form, this action is a way of protecting the ears from loud sounds, but it is also employed as a deliberate gesture to ask someone to stop making a noise.

Locality: Worldwide.

EARS COVER

Meaning: Stop that noise!

Action: The palms of the hands are pressed tightly over the ears.

Background: This is an alternative to the last gesture.

Locality: Worldwide.

EARS FAN

Meaning: Sexual insult.

Action: The tips of the little fingers are placed in the ears, with the rest of the hands fanned out sideways.

Background: This is an Arabian version of the cuckold sign. It implies that the wife of the person to whom it is directed is unfaithful. In origin, it suggests that the victim of the insult should be wearing antlers, like a stag. This contrasts with the more common cuckold sign found around the Mediterranean, where the gesturer makes a horn sign, imitating a bull. In both cases, the action implies that someone is rutting (like a bull or a stag) with the victim's wife. In the strict social world of the Arabs, this is one of the worst insults that can be thrown by one man at another. In some contexts its message would be so potent that it could easily lead to a killing.

Locality: Syria, Saudi Arabia and parts of the Lebanon.

EARS GRASP

Meaning: Remorse.

Action: The gesturer grasps his own earlobes with his hands.

Background: This is described as the action taken by a servant when being scolded for improper behaviour.

Locality: India.

EARS THUMB

Meaning: Joking insult.

Action: The thumbs are placed into the ears and the spread fingers are waggled at the victim. As an embellishment, the tongue is often protruded.

Background: This is a light-hearted insult most often used between children. It is sometimes called 'donkey ears' and is aimed at someone who has behaved stupidly, implying that they are 'like a stupid donkey with long ears.'

Locality: Widespread.

ELBOW BANG

Meaning: He is a miser.

Action: The elbow of the bent arm is banged on the table.

Background: This gesture implies that someone is mean with his money.

Locality: Common in Uruguay but also known elsewhere in Latin America.

ELBOW RAISE

Meaning: Counter-threat.

Action: The elbow, with bent arm, is quickly raised and lowered in the direction of a companion.

Background: This gesture is used when someone has been insulted or mildly threatened, suggesting that they will hit out with their elbow if they are not left in peace. It is a stylized retaliation that says 'I am not taking that!' or 'I will defend myself'. It is often accompanied by such phrases as: 'Get out of it!' or 'Clear off'.

Locality: Europe.

ELBOW TAP (1)

Meaning: Sneaky.

Action: The gesturer taps his own elbow several times with the palm of his hand.

Background: The gesture indicates that someone is underhand in their dealings.

Locality: Holland.

ELBOW TAP (2)

Meaning: You are an idiot.

Action: (As above)

Background: In this version of the gesture, the message is 'This is where you carry your brain'.

Locality: Germany and Austria.

ELBOW TAP (3)

Meaning: Mean.

Action: (As above)

Background: This version of the gesture, known locally as the 'Tacano', indicates that someone is unusually stingy and tight with money. This is a variant of the Elbow Bang gesture.

Locality: South America.

ELBOW TAP (4)

Meaning: Go to hell!

Action: The elbow of the raised forearm is tapped as the hand wags back and forth.

Background: This is an insultingly sexual version of the Italian wave, with the forearm symbolically converted into an erect penis. The right hand waves goodbye in the usual Italian style, but by slapping the left hand on to the elbow at the same time, the gesturer adds a phallic element to the signal.

Locality: Italy.

ELBOW TAP (5)

Meaning: Go to hell!

Action: The elbow of the raised forearm is tapped as the fist wags back and forth.

Background: This aggressive phallic gesture is usually made in reply to the Elbow Tap (4) gesture, the fist here giving it a more powerful, retaliatory message.

Locality: Italy.

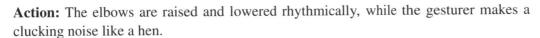

ELBOWS FLAP

Meaning: You are a coward.

Action: The elbows are raised and lowered rhythmically, while the gesturer makes a clucking noise like a hen.

Background: This is a simple mime of the flapping of the wings of a bird. The message is 'you are chicken'.

Locality: North America, but also known elsewhere.

EYE RUB (1)

Meaning: Deceit is occurring.

Action: The forefinger rubs the eye or the skin near the eye.

Background: This action is used to justify the closing of the eyes, or provide an excuse for looking away, at a moment when there is some kind of deception taking place. The gesturer urgently wants to cut off visual contact with his companion and the Eye Rub enables him to do this discreetly. Unlike the next gesture, Eye Rub (2), this action occurs without the performer being aware that he is doing it and it is therefore a useful 'telltale' sign. It may occur either when the gesturer himself is lying or when his companion is doing so. In both instances, the action makes it possible for the gesturer to avoid the companion's gaze.

Locality: Widespread.

EYE RUB (2)

Meaning: I don't care what you say.

Action: The right fist rubs the left eye.

Background: This is a gesture of indifference, performed to demonstrate that the gesturer is untouched by the critical comments being made.

Locality: Europe.

EYE 'TELESCOPE'

Meaning: She is beautiful!

Action: The hands are placed in front of one eye to make a tube, imitating the act of looking through a telescope.

Background: This is a joke imitation of the action of a Peeping Tom, usually made by one man to draw the attention of his friends to the presence of a pretty girl.

Locality: Widespread, but most common in Brazil.

EYE WINK

Meaning: Collusion.

Action: While looking at a companion, one eye is closed and then opened again.

Background: The wink is a deliberate, one-eyed blink that signals a shared secret between the winker and the winked-at. The collusion is based on the idea that the closed eye – aimed at the companion – is keeping their secret, while the open eye – aimed at the rest of the world – is excluding everyone else from the momentary intimacy. Performed between private friends it signals a moment of shared, private understanding. Performed towards a stranger it requests a shared intimacy that has yet to happen. In other words, between strangers, it becomes a flirtation signal. In books of etiquette, the wink is viewed as a vulgar gesture and it is often caricatured (when performed between strangers) as the action of a soliciting prostitute.

Locality: Western world, but increasingly widespread.

EYE WIPE

Meaning: You are making me sad.

Action: Although dry, the eye is wiped as if it is weeping.

Background: This gesture mimes the act of wiping tears from the eyes. It is most commonly seen when a parent wants to signal to a small child that it is behaving so badly that it will soon make its mother weep.

Locality: Widespread.

EYEBROW COCK

Meaning: Scepticism.

Action: One eyebrow is raised while the other remains lowered.

Background: This is a hybrid gesture, with one eye frowning and the other looking surprised. The contradictory signal – half aggressive, half scared - reflects a contradictory mood, in which the gesturer has been surprised by something, but cannot quite believe that his shock is justified.

Locality: Widespread.

EYEBROW SMOOTH

Meaning: Homosexual.

Action: The tip of the little finger is moistened on the tongue and then wiped along the eyebrow in a delicate grooming action.

Background: The delicacy of the smoothing action caricatures female cosmetic attention and implies effeminacy on the part of the male. This may be employed as a light-hearted joke or as a more serious insult.

Locality: Widespread.

EYEBROWS FLASH (I)

Meaning: Greeting.

Action: The eyebrows are rapidly raised and lowered once, in one-third of a second. The action is accompanied by a smile.

Background: This is the typical friendly greeting of all human beings, regardless of their cultural background. It is performed unconsciously and few people are aware that they are doing it. It derives from the fact that we open our eyes slightly more when we increase our attention, as we do when we meet someone. As the eyes open, so the eyebrows are raised. Then, following the moment of recognition, the eyes relax slightly and the eyebrows return to their more usual position.

Locality: Worldwide.

EYEBROWS FLASH (2)

Meaning: Flirtation.

Action: The eyebrows are raised and lowered rapidly in an exaggerated way.

Background: This is the eyebrow display that was converted in a comic cliché of flirting by Groucho Marx. It is a deliberate exaggeration of the ordinary greeting flash and is now only employed in western countries as a joke signal. In some Arab cultures however it is still seen in its original form, as a part of normal sexual flirtation.

Locality: Widespread.

EYEBROWS FLASH (3)

Meaning: No!

Action: The eyebrows are raised and lowered rapidly once. Instead of a smile, the action is accompanied by a serious or annoyed facial expression.

Background: The Greek Head Toss meaning 'No!' includes an Eyebrows Flash. Sometimes, at close quarters, the negative signal is transmitted simply by raising and lowering the eyebrows, without the usual Head Toss.

Locality: Greece.

EYEBROWS KNIT

Meaning: Acute anxiety.

Action: The eyebrows are simultaneously raised and drawn towards one another.

Background: This is a contradictory expression in which the muscles try both to raise and lower the eyebrows. The lowering action draws them together, but at the same time they press upwards. This is the expression of grief or of chronic pain, and contains elements of both fear and anger. Those individuals who experience prolonged grief maintain the expression so intensely that they eventually develop oblique eyebrows.

Locality: Worldwide.

EYELID PULL (1)

Meaning: I am alert.

Action: The tip of the forefinger touches the skin just below the eyelid and pulls it downwards, opening the eye more than usual.

Background: By emphasizing his eye, the gesturer transmits the message that he knows what is going on and that he is not being fooled. Frequently, he is implying that his companion is lying and that he does not believe him. It is an ancient gesture that has attracted many popular phrases, such as: 'There is no green in my eye', 'All my eye and Betty Martin', 'I don't have a wooden eye' and 'No sand in my eye'.

Locality: Widespread. Observed in most European countries, especially Britain, Scandinavia, Germany, Belgium, France, Portugal, Yugoslavia, Greece and Turkey.

EYELID PULL (2)

Meaning: Be alert.

Action: (As above)

Background: In this version it is not the gesturer who must be alert, but his companion. The message is 'watch out', 'keep your eyes peeled', 'there is trouble about'.

Locality: Widespread. Observed in most European countries, especially Holland, Spain and Italy. Also in Tunisia.

EYELID RUB

Meaning: Protection from the Evil Eye.

Action: The eyelid is rubbed lightly with the tip of the forefinger.

Background: This is a secretive gesture that protects the performer from someone who is feared to possess the 'Evil Eye'. In earlier centuries it was believed that certain individuals unwittingly caused havoc wherever they went, and these unfortunates were said to be possessed of evil spirits. Anything they looked upon might suffer great misfortune. As a result, many amulets were worn to protect people and specific gestures

54

were made to ward off the evil elements. This inconspicuous rubbing of the eyelid was meant to cause harm to the Evil Eye carriers, or at least to provide some sort of defence against them.

Locality: Middle East.

EYELID TOUCH (1)

Meaning: You are stupid!

Action: The tip of the right forefinger is placed on the lower eyelid of the right eye.

Background: The gesturer points to his eye, implying that he can see clearly just how stupidly the companion is behaving. This should not be confused with the very similar Eyelid Pull.

Locality: Saudi Arabia.

EYELID TOUCH (2)

Meaning: She is an eyeful!

Action: As above, but usually with a smiling face.

Background: As before, the gesturer points to his eye to emphasize that he is witnessing something of interest. In this case, the object of his gaze is an attractive female.

Locality: South America.

EYELID TOUCH (3)

Meaning: I swear!

Action: The tip of the right forefinger is placed on the upper eyelid of the right eye.

Background: An oath is sworn in a number of ways, usually by touching a vital part of the body. Here, the gesturer swears on his eye.

Locality: Saudi Arabia.

EYES 'BLIND'

Meaning: I swear it is true.

Action: Fingertips are held over the closed eyes.

Background: This is a way of swearing an oath, the
message being 'may I be struck blind if I am not telling the truth'. It plays a similar role
to the 'cross-my-heart-and-hope-to-die' gesture.

Locality: Holland.

EYES CLOSE

Meaning: Snobbery.

Action: While still looking at the companion, the eyes are closed, the eyebrows raised
and the lips pursed.

Background: The eyes are closed in a theatrical manner, with the face expressing
surprise and distaste. The signal says that something is so awful that 'I must blot it out
by shutting my eyes'. This is the snob's version of the 'Cut-off' action that is widely
employed to remove unpleasant stimuli, whether real or, as in this case, imagined.

Locality: Throughout the Western world.

EYES FLAP

Meaning: You are crazy!

Action: The flat hand is flapped up and down in front of the eyes.

Background: The gesture implies that the companion has a distorted vision of
something, the rapid movements of the hand symbolically interfering with the way they
are seeing the world.

Locality: Italy.

EYES FLUTTER

Meaning: I am innocent.

Action: The wide-open eyes blink rapidly.

Background: This is the gesture that usually provokes the response 'don't flutter your eyelashes at me!' It is used to say that 'I am wide-eyed and innocent and therefore deserve to be rewarded'. Largely a joke gesture, employed by beautiful young women towards protective men.

Locality: Western world.

EYES RAISE

Meaning: Exasperation.

Action: The eyes are rolled upwards to stare at the sky or the ceiling. The gesture is often accompanied by a clicking of the tongue.

Background: At moments of incredulity or scornful amazement, the eyes turn up to heaven as if saying 'God help me!'

Locality: Widespread.

EYES RING

Meaning: I can see you!

Action: The hands form 'spectacles' around the eyes.

Background: This gesture is used by individuals who are being scrutinized from a distance and wish to 'retaliate' in a joking way.

Locality: Widespread.

EYES SIDE-GLANCE

Meaning: I am coy.

Action: The eyes look sideways at the companion from a lowered head.

Background: This facial expression consists of two conflicting signals: (1) the bold stare, and (2) the shyly lowered head that is slightly turned away. To make it possible to stare at someone from this position, it is necessary to give them a sidelong glance. This glance, because it signals a 'bold shyness', inevitably feels strangely false. It lacks both the forthright quality of direct staring and the charming humility of shyly looking away. Its impact, therefore, is of an arch coyness, that can be either irritating or playfully appealing, according to the mood of the occasion.

Locality: Worldwide.

EYES STARE

Meaning: Threat.

Action: The eyes are opened wide by pulling back the skin all around them.

Background: The direct stare with a fixed, stony expression is always threatening. This applies to all monkeys and apes as well as to all humans. If the stare is held, without a change in facial expression, for any length of time, the person being stared at feels increasingly uncomfortable. For this reason, professional boxers often 'eyeball' one another just before a fight, in a mutual attempt to intimidate one another. The reason the stare is so worrying is because it hints at an imminent attack.

Locality: Worldwide.

EYES WEEP

Meaning: Distress.

Action: Tears spill out of the eyes and trickle down the cheeks.

Background: Monkeys and apes do not weep. Among the primates this reaction is unique to the human species. This may be because tears are highly visible on the naked skin of the human face, making weeping a powerful visual display even at a distance. On the hairy face of a monkey or an ape, the tears would be lost in the fur and there would be no display. A second function of weeping has also been suggested, namely that the tears are 'de-stressing'. We say that we feel better after 'a good cry' and there appears to be a biological basis for this statement. Studies of the chemistry of tears have shown that when we weep as a result of emotional tension, stress chemicals are present in the liquid of our tears, but when we weep merely because there is dust in our eyes, the tears contain no such chemicals. In other words, weeping rids our bodies of the excess stress chemicals that are present because of our state of misery or conflict, and it is this that improves our mood after our 'good cry'.

Locality: Worldwide.

FACE COVER

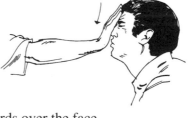

Meaning: I am shocked!

Action: The hand, with spread fingers, is brought up to cover the face.

Background: The gesture hides the face in a 'cut-off' action that 'removes' the gesturer from the offending situation. It may be performed seriously, when genuinely shocked, or it may be used in a light-hearted way when pretending to be shocked.

Locality: Widespread.

FACE DOWN-RUB

Meaning: A curse on you!

Action: The palm of the right hand is rubbed downwards over the face.

Locality: North Africa.

FACE SWIPE

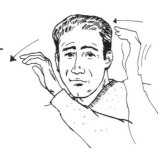

Meaning: Crazy.

Action: The hand swipes sideways in front of the face, as if snatching at something invisible.

Background: The message is that someone is out of their mind, the gesture mimicking a lunatic snatching at some imaginary object.

Locality: Holland.

FINGERNAILS POLISH

Meaning: That was clever of me!

Action: The gesturer breathes on the fingernails of one hand and then polishes them on his lapel.

Background: This act of self-congratulation, performed in jest, is seen when someone has scored a point in an argument, or some other minor social triumph. It is a stylized self-grooming action that says 'see how smart I am', the well-groomed smartness symbolizing the mental smartness in the argument.

Locality: Widespread in Europe and the Americas.

FINGERS BECKON

Meaning: Come here!

Action: The right arm is extended towards the companion with the palm of the hand facing down, and the wrist bent slightly down. The fingers are then gently fluttered in the air.

Background: The Oriental beckon, which replaces the Western, curled-forefinger beckon, may be confusing because it is so similar to the Western fingers-wave farewell. The only difference is that, with the Oriental beckon, the angle of the wrist is slightly lower. Japanese tour-guides beckoning to groups of Western clients to ask them to gather closer, are sometimes alarmed to see them respond by immediately dispersing.

Locality: Japan.

FINGERS CLAW

Meaning: Contempt.

Action: The fingers are stiffly bent like claws and the hand makes a few back and forth movements in the air.

Background: This is a mocking gesture threatening to claw at the face of the companion like a bird of prey.

Locality: Saudi Arabia.

FINGERS CLICK

Meaning: Attention.

Action: The thumb and second finger are pressed together and then snapped apart.

Background: This action – an audible gesture – draws attention to the gesturer in a variety of situations. It is employed in public places when service is required, as when gaining the attention of a waiter or impatiently asking him to hurry up. In many contexts it is considered an arrogant gesture, but in some countries it is accepted as the normal way of alerting a servant. It is also observed in a more private context when the gesturer is trying to remember something. Paradoxically, it is also used when something that has been forgotten is now suddenly remembered. It is an early gesture known from ancient Rome, when its main function was calling servants to approach at table.

Locality: Widespread in the Western world and the Middle East.

FINGERS COOL

Meaning: Flirtation.

Action: The fingers are swung loosely back and forth in the air, as if trying to cool them down.

Background: The gesture mimes the act of cooling the fingers after they have touched something very hot. It is performed by a man when he sees a woman who is imagined to be so 'hot' that it would burn him just to touch her. This gesture should not be confused with the Fingers Shake that signals regret. In the flirtation gesture the hand moves much more slowly through the air. In the regret gesture the action is more agitated.

Locality: Common in Europe, especially Italy.

FINGERS CROSS (1)

Meaning: Protection.

Action: The middle finger is twisted around the forefinger. The other fingers are held down by the thumb.

Background: This is a stylized way of making the sign of the cross. By crossing the fingers, the gesturer asks for the protection of the Christian deity. It is such an extreme modification of the full sign-of-the-cross that its religious origins are usually overlooked and it is now used by non-Christians as well as Christians, as a way of saying 'good luck'. The phrase that often accompanies it is 'I am keeping my fingers crossed for you', meaning 'I hope you come to no harm', or 'I hope you do well'. If the gesturer wishes to protect himself – as when telling a lie – he may make the sign with his hand held out of sight of his companion. A common version of this sees the gesturer holding his hand, with fingers crossed, behind his own back.

Locality: Widespread in Christian countries. The areas where it is most popular are the British Isles and Scandinavia.

FINGERS CROSS (2)

Meaning: Friendship.

Action: (As above)

Background: Here the two entwined fingers symbolize the closeness of two friends.

Locality: Widespread.

FINGERS CROSS (3)

Meaning: Threat to end friendship.

Action: (As above)

Background: Wherever the crossed fingers represent friendship they can also signal the end of friendship. This is usually done by first crossing the fingers and then flicking them apart. But if someone is not actually ending a friendship, but only threatening to do so, he may hold up his crossed fingers as if *about* to flick them apart.

Locality: Southern Italy and the eastern Mediterranean, especially Turkey.

FINGERS FLEX (1)

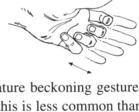

Meaning: Money.

Action: The fingers open and close repeatedly.

Background: The opening and closing of the hand is a miniature beckoning gesture, asking for the money to come closer. As a request for money, this is less common than the Fingertips Rub.

Locality: South America.

FINGERS FLEX (2)

Meaning: Money.

Action: As above, but with the hand raised to head height.

Background: (As above)

Locality: South America.

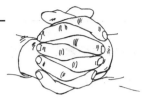

FINGERS INTERLOCK (1)

Meaning: I swear.

Action: The fingers are interlocked and held forward in front of the body.

Locality: Burma.

FINGERS INTERLOCK (2)

Meaning: Be merciful.

Action: The fingers are interlocked and the hands rocked up and down by a wrist action.

Background: This is an anguished version of a common posture of prayer. In the ordinary prayer posture the hands are held still in front of the body instead of being moved up and down. This position of the hands imitates the bound wrists of a captive who is begging for mercy.

Locality: Widespread.

FINGERS SHAKE

Meaning: Regret.

Action: The loosely held fingers are shaken up and down vigorously several times.

Background: This gesture should not be confused with the much slower Fingers Cool used as a flirtation signal.

Locality: South America.

FINGERS SHUT

Meaning: Shut up!

Action: The hand is held up and the fingers are snapped down against the thumb.

Background: The hand mimes the action of a mouth shutting tight.

Locality: France.

FINGERS SPREAD (1)

Meaning: He is stupid.

Action: The hand is held out, palm up, and then the fingers are all spread out fully.

Background: This is an exaggerated version of the simple Hands Shrug, employed in situations that cause exasperation.

Locality: South America.

FINGERS SPREAD (2)

Meaning: Insult.

Action: The hand is raised with the fingers spread wide, but the thumb folded in.

Background: For the Japanese the four-fingers gesture is a powerful insult because it suggests that the victim is a member of the outcast class called 'eta'. These people, scorned by other Japanese, were forced to undertake the more unsavoury tasks, in slaughterhouses and butchers' shops, and as a result became associated with four-legged animals. The four fingers of the gesture symbolize the four legs of these animals. The insult therefore says: 'You are a worthless outcast fit only to perform menial tasks with four-legged animals.'

Locality: Japan.

FINGERS STEEPLE

Meaning: I am thinking.

Action: The fingertips are brought together and the lips are rested on the tips of the forefingers.

Background: The gesture has (1) an element of prayer that gives it a peaceful quality suitable for deep thought, (2) a bodily symmetry that aids contemplation, (3) a protective element in that it forms a barrier across the front of the body, and (4) an oral-contact element that makes it comforting. It is this combination that makes it so popular as a 'thinker's posture'.

Locality: Widespread.

FINGERS 'TALK' (I)

Meaning: Chatterbox.

Action: With the hand held out, palms down, the fingers and thumb open and close.

Background: This is a simple mime of human jaws opening and closing. It is used to comment on someone who is talking too much or too long, or who is gossiping too much.

Locality: Widespread.

FINGERS 'TALK' (2)

Meaning: (As above)

Action: The forefinger and middle finger open and close rapidly several times. The hand may move slightly away from the body as this happens.

Background: This is a local variant of the gesture, in which only two fingers are employed to mimic the opening and closing of the jaws of the gossip. Some people have interpreted this gesture differently as 'scissors cutting off yards of nothing' and others have referred to it as the 'goose's mouth', but regardless of the precise symbolism involved in the origin of the gesture, its popularity is undoubtedly due to the chattering, 'yakity-yak' quality of its finger actions.

Locality: Italy.

FINGERS WAVE (1)

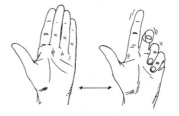

Meaning: Hallo or goodbye.

Action: The hand is held up, palm showing, and then the four fingers are bent and straightened in synchrony, as a unit, several times.

Background: This is a gentle version of the wave, used at close quarters, especially when saying goodbye to children. It is a mime of patting a child on the head, performed at long distance.

Locality: Widespread.

FINGERS WAVE (2)

Meaning: Hallo or goodbye.

Action: As above, but the fingers are not waved as a unit. Instead, they are waggled repeatedly in sequence.

Background: As above. This version of the gesture can be confused with the Japanese Fingers Beckon. The only difference is that, in the beckon, the hand is held slightly lower.

Locality: Widespread.

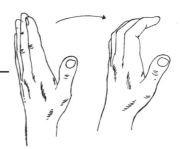

FINGERS WAVE (3)

Meaning: Hallo or goodbye.

Action: The hand is held up, palm hidden, and then the four fingers are bent and straightened in synchrony, as a unit, several times.

Background: This is the 'Italian Wave' and is easily confused with the palm-up Hand Beckon (1). In origin, it is a long-distance pat on the back.

Locality: Italy, including Sicily and Sardinia.

FINGERTIPS FAN

Meaning: Go away!

Action: The bunched fingertips are directed at the onlooker and are then fanned out quickly, like a flower opening its petals.

Background: This is the stylized version of the more usual Hand Flick that is used to tell someone to clear off.

Locality: Egypt.

FINGERTIPS KISS (1)

Meaning: Praise.

Action: The fingertips are lightly touched to the lips and the hand is then tossed away from the mouth. As the hand moves away, the bunched fingers are spread.

Background: This is an ancient gesture, known for over 2000 years. The early Greeks and Romans were in the habit of throwing a kiss towards the image of a deity when entering or leaving a temple. Its original message was 'adoration', and it was employed only in sacred contexts, but as time passed its use spread to any form of praise, adulation or flattery. Given to high-status humans, its message became 'You are so god-like that I offer you this sacred salutation.' It remained a courtly gesture for many centuries and was seen as a foppish affectation by those outside court circles. By the eighteenth century it had become reduced to a mere flourish of the hand in which the lips were no longer touched, but in modern times it returned in its full form in a new context. This occurred when it spread from the formal to the informal sphere. In a playful way, it became the gesture to express admiration, not for a god or an emperor, but for a tasty morsel of food or an exciting work of art. In all its various forms, however, it retains one common feature: it is the kiss offered to the person or object that cannot be given the usual, direct, kissing mouth contact.

Locality: Widespread, although often caricatured as a flowery French or 'Continental' gesture.

FINGERTIPS KISS (2)

Meaning: Salutation.

Action: (As above)

Background: In certain parts of Europe, the kissing of the fingertips towards another person is used as a salutation, rather than as praise. In ancient times it was both at once, the gesturer greeting and praising simultaneously. Today, in its modern, informal contexts, the ancient double message has split into two. There is a small difference between the two: when used as praise it is not always directed at the object in question; when used as a salutation it is always aimed at the person being greeted. In its salutation role it may be used either as a greeting or as a farewell gesture.

Locality: Although widespread, it is only common in certain regions. For some reason it is most popular on islands (Malta, Sicily, Sardinia, and Corfu). On the mainland it is a common salutation in Portugal (but not Spain) and Sweden (but not Denmark). This is a strange distribution that has yet to be explained.

FINGERTIPS KISS (3)

Meaning: I love you.

Action: The fingertips are kissed lightly, as above, but with a flatter hand. The hand is then lowered into a palm-up position and the mouth 'blows' the kiss towards the loved one.

Background: A playful way of sending a long-distance kiss to someone who is too far away for a full mouth contact. Most often directed towards a child or a lover. It may appear in an abbreviated form, with the kissed fingertips merely being raised towards the companion, with the blowing element omitted. This milder form is often used between elderly companions with reduced mobility.

Locality: Widespread.

FINGERTIPS RUB

Meaning: Money.

Action: Rubbing the fingertips with the thumb of the same hand.

Background: The gesture may be a simple request for money or a reference to the fact that something is being done merely for the monetary reward involved. It is based on a mime of feeling a coin between the fingers and thumb.

Locality: Widespread.

FINGERTIPS SQUEEZE

Meaning: You are a coward!

Action: The hand mimes the action of squeezing something soft.

Background: The symbolism of this gesture is simple – the squeezing of something soft implies that the person at whom the action is directed is 'soft', in other words, spineless and cowardly.

Locality: Gypsy communities.

FINGERTIPS STRUM

Meaning: I am impatient.

Action: The fingertips are strummed on a convenient surface.

Background: This unconscious action frequently occurs when someone has been kept waiting, or is impatient that something is not happening. It is a symbolic form of 'running away'. In evolutionary terms, our hands were once our front feet and, even today, whenever we wish to depart but cannot do so for some reason, we start to fidget with our fingers. Their urgent movements represent the relic of our urge to get up and go. This is similar to a bull pawing the ground before charging. Our hand makes the small 'intention movements' of locomotion, reflecting our true mood.

Locality: Worldwide.

FINGERTIPS TOUCH

Meaning: I may make a journey.

Action: With eyes closed, the hands are brought into contact with one another, fingertips to fingertips.

Background: This is a gesture used as an omen. If the fingertips fail to touch, no trip is undertaken.

Locality: Bedouin tribes.

FIST BEAT

Meaning: Victory.

Action: The clenched fist is raised high in the air and then delivers a powerful beat, forward and downward. It is often accompanied by a leap into the air.

Background: This is a popular victory gesture of uninhibited sportsmen. It is derived from the primeval overarm blow that is common to all mankind. The gesture symbolically says 'my strength has overcome my enemy.'

Locality: Largely confined to Western sportsmen.

FIST CLENCH (I)

Meaning: Power.

Action: The clenched fist is raised in front of the body.

Background: This clenched fist gesture mimics the power-grip position of the hand. When a clenched fist accompanies speech it helps to make a forceful point. This has been stylized in the form of the Communist salute. It is also frequently used by victorious sportsmen as a sign of triumph. In its sporting context it is a weaker form of the Fist Beat.

Locality: Widespread.

FIST CLENCH (2)

Meaning: Stingy.

Action: The clenched fist is held in front of the body.

Background: The clenched fist held close in front of the body indicates that someone is 'tight-fisted', or mean, and should not be confused with the raised fist that signifies power or anger.

Locality: Japan.

FIST CLENCH (3)

Meaning: Obscene insult.

Action: The clenched fist is displayed towards a companion.

Background: In many places a jerked fist is considered an obscene gesture, but in some regions even the unjerked fist is seen as a sexual insult.

Locality: Pakistan.

FIST JERK

Meaning: Masturbation.

Action: The loose fist is moved up and down rapidly in front of the body.

Background: This gesture, which is a simple mime of male masturbation, is frequently seen at British football matches, where it is simultaneously used by large sections of the crowd when an opposing player has failed spectacularly in some attempt.

Locality: Western world.

FIST PUMP

Meaning: Like hell!

Action: The clenched fist is pumped forwards and backwards several times.

Background: This is an insulting way of saying 'no' in response to a question that annoys the gesturer.

Locality: South America.

FIST PUNCH

Meaning: Forceful emphasis.

Action: A speaker punches the air with his clenched fist.

Background: Angry or belligerent speakers often emphasize their words with a raised fist, symbolically delivering a beating to any opposition there might be to their ideas. Although frequently used unconsciously in the heat of debate, this action is so well known that it is often used by meek-and-mild speakers who wish to give the impression of being more forceful than they really are.

Locality: Worldwide, especially in political circles.

FIST RAISE

Meaning: Victory!

Action: The clenched fist is raised high into the air on a straight arm.

Background: This is the frozen version of the overarm beat, with the fist raised as if to strike down, but instead held still at the highest point of the movement.

FIST SHAKE (1)

Meaning: Threat.

Action: With the face glaring angrily, the clenched fist is shaken rapidly backwards and forwards in the direction of the other person.

Background: This 'Intention Movement' of hitting someone is the most commonly observed threat display of our species. Although there are many other local insult displays and threatening actions, the Fist Shake is performed and understood everywhere.

Locality: Worldwide.

FIST SHAKE (2)

Meaning: We won!

Action: The clenched fist is raised above the head and is then shaken back and forth, while the face shows intense pleasure.

Background: This is a cheerful, symbolic beating of the defeated rivals with the right fist. Most commonly observed at sporting or political events.

Locality: Widespread.

FIST SIDE-SHAKE

Meaning: Fight.

Action: The clenched fist is held slightly to one side at shoulder level and then moved from side to side several times.

Background: This is a stylized form of fist-shaking in which the movement is performed sideways instead of the usual forward and backward, making it more visible to the onlooker.

Locality: Colombia.

FIST SLAP

Meaning: Sexual insult.

Action: The fist of one hand is slapped hard against the palm of the other. This is done rhythmically several times.

Background: The gesture mimics the pounding beat of pelvic thrusting during copulation. The colloquial message is 'Up yours!'

Locality: Most commonly observed in Italy, but also seen in France, Spain and South America. In North America this gesture is sometimes used casually without any specific, insulting significance and this can cause confusion where visitors are concerned.

FIST TWIST

Meaning: Threat to evil spirits.

Action: The fist is held against the lips and rotated through a half-turn.

Background: Used by women to protect themselves against 'jinn', or unseen evil spirits.

Locality: Saudi Arabia.

FISTS CLENCH

Meaning: I will strangle you.

Action: Both fists are clenched and raised together, with the thumbs pointing outwards, away from the body.

Background: This action mimics the pulling tight of an (invisible) rope around the neck of an offender.

Locality: Syria.

FISTS DIP

Meaning: Good luck.

Action: The fists, with thumbs hidden, are dipped downwards with a short jerk.

Background: Hiding or holding the thumbs for good luck is an alternative to the more widespread 'keeping your fingers crossed' gesture, used as a protection against bad luck.

Locality: Germany.

FISTS RAISE

Meaning: Victory.

Action: The clenched fists are raised high in the air.

Background: This is a slightly more belligerent version of the triumphant Arms Raise (3) gesture, popular with sportsmen whose activities involve fairly aggressive encounters.

Locality: Widespread.

FISTS WRING

Meaning: Anger.

Action: The fists mime the action of twisting a wet cloth to squeeze the water out of it.

Background: The message is obvious enough – I would like to wring your neck. It is often used as a threat that revenge will be taken, following some wrong-doing, but it is largely confined to children. When used by adults it is usually in a joking context.

Locality: Europe and the Americas.

FOOT JIGGLE

Meaning: I am bored.

Action: The foot of a seated person is jigged rapidly up and down in the air.

Background: Like the Fingers Strum and the Foot Tap, this is a sign that someone wants to escape. The jigging movements of the foot are token 'running away' actions. But because the foot movements of the Foot Jiggle can be greatly reduced until they become almost imperceptible, this action is often less aggressively rude than overt finger strumming or foot tapping.

Locality: Worldwide.

FOOT KISS

Meaning: Humble salutation.

Action: The companion's foot is kissed.

Background: With all kissing, the lower the kiss is applied, the greater the sign of respect and humble submission. Kissing the hand is more respectful than kissing the cheek, and kissing the foot is even more cringingly subordinate. The phrase 'kiss the dirt' originated from the fact that certain individuals were too lowly even to kiss the feet of a dominant individual, and had to make do with kissing the ground near his feet. In today's (officially) egalitarian societies, the Foot Kiss is an extreme rarity, but it still survives in a ritual form when the Pope symbolically washes and kisses the feet of poor people in Holy Week. This is to demonstrate that, despite the pomp and grandeur of his office, he is at heart a truly humble Christian.

Locality: Vatican City.

FOOT LOCK (I)

Meaning: Discomfort.

Action: One foot locks itself firmly around the back of the other leg. The figure is seated.

Background: This unconscious action is a telltale sign that someone is feeling nervous or uncomfortable, no matter how relaxed the upper parts of the body may appear. Generally speaking, our feet are the most honest part of our bodies. This is because we are less aware of them than the parts nearer the face. People engaged in friendly conversation often look completely at ease, but their feet give them away. The Foot Lock gives them a sense of security because it acts as an 'anchor', holding them firmly in place.

Locality: Worldwide.

FOOT LOCK (2)

Meaning: (As above)

Action: One foot locks itself around the back of the other leg. The figure is standing.

Background: This version of the gesture is performed almost exclusively by women. Although it has the same background as the seated Foot Lock, it is a more difficult posture to maintain, leaving the person concerned poised awkwardly on one leg. Despite this it obviously provides sufficient 'security' to justify its existence.

Locality: Worldwide.

FOOT SHOW

Meaning: Insult.

Action: A sitting or reclining person shows the sole of his shoe to his companion.

Background: In certain countries, if this is done accidentally, it can cause serious trouble. People have even been murdered for showing the sole of a shoe to someone. Special care has to be taken when sitting with crossed legs, or when putting one's feet up on a chair or desk. If it is thought to be a deliberate action, a major fracas may follow. Recently, a Thai cabaret singer shot a client who sat with the sole of his shoe pointing at the stage. The reason this simple action is considered particularly insulting is that the bottom of the shoe is seen as the lowliest part of the body, the part that steps in dirt.

Locality: The Middle East and parts of the Orient. This gesture is especially powerful in Saudi Arabia, Egypt, Singapore and Thailand.

FOOT TAP

Meaning: I am impatient.

Action: The foot is tapped rhythmically on the ground.

Background: This has the same message as the Fingers Strum and Foot Jiggle gestures. The foot makes the movements of running away, but the body stays where it is. In other words, it is a stylized escape movement reduced to a relic, and performed whenever the person concerned would rather be somewhere else but cannot, for social reasons, bring himself to depart.

Locality: Widespread.

FOREARM CLASP

Meaning: Greeting.

Action: Two men simultaneously grasp one another's forearms with their right hands.

Background: This was the typical greeting of the ancient Romans and was their version of today's Hand Shake. It was a mutual display of friendliness based on the non-aggressive use (and momentary incapacitation) of the sword-hand.

Locality: Common in Ancient Rome, rare today.

FOREARM JERK (1)

Meaning: Sexual insult.

Action: The clenched right fist is jerked upwards. Its progress is forcibly halted by slapping the left hand down on the crook of the bent right arm. A variant form sees the forearm shot forward instead of jerked upwards.

Background: This is a popular phallic gesture, with the right forearm acting as a symbolic penis becoming erect. In some countries (such as Malta) it is illegal to perform this gesture in a public place. There the gesturer makes only the merest suggestion of performing the Forearm Jerk. He does this by rubbing his upper forearm, suggesting the full gesture that might have been.

Locality: Widespread, but less common in the far north of Europe than elsewhere. In Hungary, the phallus formed by the Forearm Jerk is specifically named as belonging to a horse, making the sexual assault of the gesture more extreme.

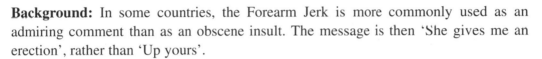

FOREARM JERK (2)

Meaning: Sexual comment.

Action: (As above)

Background: In some countries, the Forearm Jerk is more commonly used as an admiring comment than as an obscene insult. The message is then 'She gives me an erection', rather than 'Up yours'.

Locality: Common only in the British Isles, but also occasionally encountered elsewhere.

FOREARM THRUST (1)

Meaning: Sexual insult.

Action: The clenched fist knuckle up, is thrust forward (instead of being jerked upwards). Its progress forward is forcibly halted by slapping the left hand down on the crook of the right arm.

Background: This is a variant of the ordinary Forearm Jerk (1), ending with a straight arm instead of a bent one. Symbolically, it replaces the 'erection' element with an 'insertion' one.

Locality: Italy.

FOREARM THRUST (2)

Meaning: Sexual insult.

Action: As above, except that the hand is flat instead of being clenched into a fist.

Background: This is another local variation of the phallic insult gesture.

Locality: Italy.

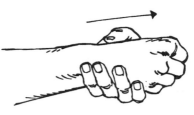

FOREARM THRUST (3)

Meaning: Sexual insult.

Action: The right fist is thrust forward through the loosely curled left hand. The movement is halted by the action of grabbing the right forearm with the left hand.

Background: The forearm is acting as a symbolic penis being thrust into an orifice. It is a local variation of the more widespread Forearm Jerk.

Locality: Lebanon and Syria.

FOREFINGER BEAT

Meaning: Moderate threat.

Action: The raised forefinger repeatedly beats downward in the direction of the companion.

Background: The stiff finger is acting like a miniature club with which the speaker symbolically beats the companion over the head. This is a gesture much favoured by headmasters, politicians and other speakers in a strongly authoritarian mood. It is usually an unconscious gesticulation of which the speaker is barely aware.

Locality: Worldwide.

FOREFINGER BECKON

Meaning: Come here.

Action: With the hand held palm-up and all the other fingers closed, the forefinger beckons by curling and uncurling several times.

Background: This form of beckoning is used in the West at close quarters. It may be used archly in a flirtatious encounter, or may be used sarcastically in a 'schoolteacherish' manner.

Locality: Widespread.

FOREFINGER BITE (I)

Meaning: I am angry.

Action: The knuckle of the bent forefinger is placed between the teeth and symbolically bitten.

Background: This is an example of redirected aggression in which the enraged person does to himself what he would like to do to the onlooker.

Locality: Italy.

FOREFINGER BITE (2)

Meaning: I am sorry.

Action: The middle joint of the bent forefinger is symbolically bitten.

Background: Here the gesture is based on the idea of a token self-punishment when making an apology. This gesture could easily be confused with the previous one, with disastrous results.

Locality: Saudi Arabia.

82

FOREFINGER BITE (3)

Meaning: Lucky.

Action: The forefinger is placed sideways in the mouth, bitten, then removed and shaken.

Background: This version of the forefinger bite is based on the idea that the 'attacked' finger is lucky enough to escape.

Locality: Lebanon, Syria and Saudi Arabia.

FOREFINGER BLOW

Meaning: Be quiet!

Action: The forefinger is brought close to the mouth. The gesturer blows on it.

Background: This is a local variant of the more familiar 'Lips Touch' request for silence.

Locality: Saudi Arabia.

FOREFINGER CROOK

Meaning: He is not a Moslem.

Action: The forefinger is bent tightly on itself in a crook shape.

Locality: Saudi Arabia.

FOREFINGER CROSS

Meaning: I swear.

Action: The stiff forefinger traces the sign of a Christian cross in the air.

Background: This is the sign of the cross that is usually performed with the first and second finger together, as a priest's blessing, but is here made with the forefinger alone.

Locality: Italy.

FOREFINGER DIP

Meaning: No.

Action: The slightly curled forefinger is dipped downwards.

Background: The hand makes the downward 'nod' more usually performed by the head.

Locality: North America (Indian tribes).

FOREFINGER EXTEND

Meaning: Small.

Action: The stiff forefinger is extended horizontally, with the thumb resting on the first joint.

Background: This is less common than its Little-Finger equivalent, for the obvious reason that the little finger is the smallest of the digits.

Locality: Italy, the Middle East and South America.

FOREFINGER HOOK

Meaning: Thief.

Action: The forefinger is held briefly in a hooked position.

Background: The gesture mimes the act of a thief hooking away someone's possessions.

Locality: Japan.

FOREFINGER HOP

Meaning: Tomorrow.

Action: The stiff forefinger is looped upward and forward in a semi-circular movement.

Background: The finger describes a forward motion, as if turning a page of time, or following the course of the sun. If the gesturer is referring to 'the day after tomorrow' the forefinger makes two loops, the second in front of the first. In less precise contexts the gesture may simply mean 'later on'.

Locality: Widespread, but most common in the Mediterranean region.

FOREFINGER INSERT

Meaning: Copulation.

Action: The stiff forefinger is inserted into a ring formed by the other hand. It is then moved in and out of the opening in a rhythmic way.

Background: This is a simple mime of the insertion of the penis into the vagina. Its symbolism is so basic that it is widely understood, even by travellers from regions where it is not commonly employed. It is used either as a deliberately offensive obscenity, or as an uninhibited invitation to sex.

Locality: Widespread. Known throughout Europe, the Middle East and the Americas.

FOREFINGER KISS

Meaning: I offer you a kiss.

Action: The tip of the finger is kissed.

Background: This is a variant of the more common Fingertips Kiss, in which the gesturer performs a long-distance kiss. In this case, he uses only his forefinger tip as the substitute for the object or person he wishes to praise or greet.

Locality: Southern Italy.

FOREFINGER LICK

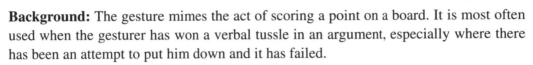

Meaning: One up to me.

Action: The forefinger is licked briefly and then draws an imaginary figure 1 in the air.

Background: The gesture mimes the act of scoring a point on a board. It is most often used when the gesturer has won a verbal tussle in an argument, especially where there has been an attempt to put him down and it has failed.

Locality: Western world.

FOREFINGER POINT (1)

Meaning: Indicates direction.

Action: The forefinger points in a specific direction, usually in response to a query.

Background: Although we take for granted the action of giving hand-signal directions to companions, this is a uniquely human activity. A few other animals are able to indicate direction in various ways, (bees dance in their hive and wolves point with their whole bodies, for example) but only humans perform accurate finger-pointing. This became an important gesture for our species when we evolved into cooperative hunters. The silent indication of direction must then have been vital to the success of many a stealthy pursuit of prey. Among surviving hunters today, there is a refinement of the pointing action, to indicate not only direction but also distance. This is done by raising the angle of the pointing forefinger to suggest increased distance, as if the finger is an arrow about to be fired at a target.

Locality: Worldwide.

FOREFINGER POINT (2)

Meaning: Threat.

Action: The forefinger points directly at the companion.

Background: The direct forefinger point is used at moments of anger during verbal exchanges. Its threatening quality stems from the sensation that the stiff finger is a symbolic weapon, about to stab the victim. For this reason, children are often instructed that 'It is rude to point.'

Locality: Worldwide.

FOREFINGER PRESS

Meaning: I curse you!

Action: The forefinger is held down by the thumb.

Background: This gesture makes the sign of the cross, formed between the thumb and forefinger, the implication being that the other person is so evil that the gesturer needs holy protection. It is related to the Thumbnail Kiss, used when swearing an oath. The difference is that here only the second half of that gesture is performed.

Locality: Spain.

FOREFINGER RAISE (1)

Meaning: Excuse me!

Action: The hand is raised, with the palm facing the companion, and the forefinger is held erect. This position may be held for some time, until it is finally acknowledged.

Background: It is used in classrooms to gain the attention of the teacher, and in restaurants to attract the attention of the waiter.

Locality: Widespread.

FOREFINGER RAISE (2)

Meaning: God is my witness.

Action: The forefinger is raised high in the air.

Background: This gesture has been used by various religious groups as a way of signalling their faith. By pointing up to the heavens, they are symbolically putting themselves 'in touch' with their god.

Locality: Widespread.

FOREFINGER RAISE (3)

Meaning: I am Number One!

Action: (As above)

Background: At moments of triumph, sportsmen use this gesture to confirm that they have just won. Here the finger symbolizes the number 1.

Locality: Western countries.

FOREFINGER RAISE (4)

Meaning: Pay attention!

Action: The stiff forefinger is raised in the air and held there. The arm does not, however, thrust upward, so that the finger is in front of the face rather than above it. Also, the palm faces sideways, instead of towards the companion.

Background: This is a domineering gesture with the forefinger acting as a symbolic club, raised and ready to strike if necessary.

Locality: Worldwide.

FOREFINGER SLOT

Meaning: Sexual comment.

Action: The right hand is slapped into the left hand so that its stiff forefinger slots in between the left thumb and forefinger.

Background: The action mimes the placing of the phallus in the slot of the female genitals.

Locality: South America.

FOREFINGER STAB

Meaning: I defy you.

Action: The right forefinger stabs through a finger-V made by the left hand.

Background: Although this may have a sexual origin, with the message 'I will rape you', to some gesturers it may be no more than a simple body-stabbing action, threatening violent assault of a non-sexual nature.

Locality: Jordan and Lebanon.

FOREFINGER STRADDLE

Meaning: Insult.

Action: The left forefinger is straddled by an inverted-V made of the first two fingers of the right hand.

Background: The gesture mimes the act of riding. The inverted-V of two fingers represents the legs of the rider and the meaning of the insult is 'I will ride you like a donkey'.

Locality: Saudi Arabia.

FOREFINGER SUCK (1)

Meaning: Regret.

Action: The tip of the bent forefinger is placed between the lips and kept there for a while, as the person thinks.

Background: This is a relic gesture in which the finger-sucker reverts momentarily to the childhood comfort of oral contact. It is, in effect, an adult version of thumb-sucking.

Locality: Widespread.

FOREFINGER SUCK (2)

Meaning: I have no money left.

Action: The straight forefinger is placed in the mouth, sucked briefly and then withdrawn.

Locality: Arab countries.

FOREFINGER TIPS-TOUCH

Meaning: You have five fathers.

Action: The right forefinger is tapped lightly on the bunched fingertips of the left hand.

Background: This deeply offensive Arab insult implies that the onlooker's mother is a whore or, at best, highly promiscuous. With so many men in her bed it is impossible for her son to tell which one is the true father. In the symbolism of the gesture, the five digits on the left hand represent the 'five fathers' and the right forefinger stands for the son.

Locality: Saudi Arabia.

FOREFINGER WAG

Meaning: No!

Action: The erect forefinger is wagged from side to side.

Background: This is a digital version of the lateral head-shake and carries the same negative message. It often has the special flavour of a mild reprimand: 'Naughty, naughty, must not do that.'

Locality: Widespread.

FOREFINGER-AND-MIDDLE-FINGER CROSS

Meaning: I swear.

Action: The first two fingers from each hand are crossed over one another.

Background: Forming the Christian cross is a commonly observed way of making an oath binding. This is sometimes done by kissing crossed forefingers, but in this instance the hands are held in front of the body.

Locality: Southern Italy.

FOREFINGER-AND-MIDDLE-FINGER POINT

Meaning: Bang, you're dead.

Action: The hand mimes the shape of a pistol and pretends to fire at the companion.

Background: This mock shooting of a friend is employed in a friendly way when he has done something foolish. It should not be confused with the following gesture.

Locality: Widespread.

FOREFINGER-AND-MIDDLE-FINGER RAISE

Meaning: Blessing.

Action: The hand is held up, palm showing, with the thumb and the first two fingers erect and the other fingers bent.

Background: This is an ancient hand position with a long history, known as the 'Mano Pantea'. It is still employed today by the Catholic Church when bestowing a blessing. According to one theory it owes its origin to the idea that the thumb and the first two fingers together symbolize the Holy Trinity. According to another it is a gesture that displays 'non-action' because the fingers are in a position that immobilizes the hand, making it impossible for it either to grip or to push. It is claimed that this gives the gesture an air of serenity and benign peacefulness.

Locality: Catholic countries.

FOREFINGER-AND-MIDDLE-FINGER SHOW

Meaning: Friendship.

Action: The first two fingers are shown to the companion held stiffly pressed together.

Background: The two fingers represent the two friends and the closeness of the fingers symbolizes the tight bond that exists between the two individuals. The gesture is usually made without pointing the fingers directly at the companion, in order to avoid confusion with the previous gesture.

Locality: Saudi Arabia.

FOREFINGER-AND-MIDDLE-FINGER 'SMOKE'

Meaning: Do you have a cigarette?

Action: The first two fingers are raised near the mouth, while the lips mime the action of pulling on a cigarette.

Background: Because it is a simple mime, this gesture is understood almost everywhere in the world. In some countries it may be confused with the V-for-victory signal or, more unfortunately, with the British insult-V.

Locality: Worldwide except for non-smoking cultures.

FOREFINGER-AND-MIDDLE-FINGER STAB

Meaning: Threat.

Action: The separated forefinger and the middle finger are stabbed towards the companion's eyes.

Background: This gesture says 'I will poke your eyes out' and is used both as a serious threat and also as a mild, almost joking insult during an argument.

Locality: Widespread.

FOREFINGER-AND-MIDDLE-FINGER THRUST

Meaning: Go halfway to hell.

Action: The first two fingers are thrust vigorously towards the companion, as if pushing something into his face.

Background: This is the Half-Moutza employed as a gross insult. Its origin is the same as the Palm Thrust in which the whole hand is pushed forward.

Locality: Greece.

FOREFINGERS AIM

Meaning: Disagreement.

Action: The forefingers are pointed at one another and then jerked back and forth.

Background: The forefingers symbolize two enemies or opposing elements. In Spanish the gesture is known as 'De punta', or 'at odds'.

Locality: Spain and the Spanish-speaking Americas.

FOREFINGERS CONTACT (I)

Meaning: Agreed!

Action: The forefingers are pressed together, side by side.

Background: The forefingers represent two individuals who have come together on a business issue.

Locality: Middle East.

FOREFINGERS CONTACT (2)

Meaning: Close friends.

Action: (As above)

Background: Here, the two forefingers stand for two friends who have come very close together, possibly as lovers.

Locality: North Africa.

FOREFINGERS HOOK (1)

Meaning: Enemies.

Action: The forefingers are hooked together.

Background: This gesture is easily confused with Forefingers Hook (2). In this case, the hooking of the fingers is seen as a preparation for tearing them apart, as in the gesture Forefingers Unhook. It signals 'enemies' because it threatens what will come. But it looks the same as the joining of fingers in friendship, so that mistakes can easily be made.

Locality: Morocco.

FOREFINGERS HOOK (2)

Meaning: We are friends.

Action: Two children join forefingers and hold them hooked together for a moment.

Background: This is a small ritual that acts as a declaration of friendship. As a variant, it may also be performed with the little fingers. It should not be confused with the previous gesture.

Locality: Widespread.

FOREFINGERS LINK

Meaning: Marriage.

Action: The forefingers are linked, with one pulling the other backwards.

Background: This is a variant of the Forefingers Hook (2) gesture, but here it is performed by one person instead of two. The tight linking of the two fingers symbolizes the powerful bond between the married man and woman.

Locality: South America.

FOREFINGERS RUB (1)

Meaning: Friendship.

Action: The forefingers are extended and rubbed together.

Background: In the language of gestures, the forefinger is often used to signify the 'self'. It follows that friendship can be signalled by bringing together two forefingers in some way, either one from each of two friends, or both from one person, as in this case. This is a variant of the Forefingers Contact (2) gesture, with a little friendly rubbing added.

Locality: Middle East.

FOREFINGERS RUB (2)

Meaning: Shame on you!

Action: One forefinger is rubbed up and down the other.

Background: Here the rubbing of the two fingers symbolizes friction.

Locality: North America.

FOREFINGERS SCRAPE (1)

Meaning: Insult.

Action: One forefinger is repeatedly scraped with the other.

Background: The action is slightly different from the one in the previous gesture, the active, scraping finger 'sawing' the other finger, rather than rubbing up and down along its length. But again, it appears to symbolize friction.

Locality: Wales, Germany and Austria.

FOREFINGERS SCRAPE (2)

Meaning: Bribe.

Action: The right forefinger 'saws' across the top of the extended left forefinger, as if cutting it in half.

Background: This gesture is very similar to the previous one but seems to have a different origin. Here, the symbolism is: 'I will split it with you, half for you and half for me'.

Locality: Colombia.

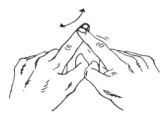

FOREFINGERS 'SHARPEN'

Meaning: Insult.

Action: One forefinger is stropped on the other, as if sharpening a knife.

Background: This is used as a symbolic threat in a juvenile context.

Locality: Holland.

FOREFINGERS TAP (1)

Meaning: Strained relations.

Action: The forefingers are tapped together rapidly.

Background: The gesture is used when social tensions arise and when the spoken word might make matters worse.

Locality: Japan.

FOREFINGERS TAP (2)

Meaning: Come to bed with me.

Action: The forefingers are held side-by-side and tapped together.

Background: Here the fingers represent the man and the woman making rhythmic, sexual contact with one another.

Locality: Egypt.

FOREFINGERS TAP (3)

Meaning: Marriage.

Action: The forefingers are knocked together.

Background: This is similar to the previous gesture but is used more as a comment concerning an existing relationship, rather than an invitation.

Locality: Southern Italy and Greece.

FOREFINGERS UNHOOK

Meaning: Our friendship is at an end.

Action: The forefingers are linked then forcibly pulled apart.

Background: This movement is the symbolic breaking of a pact. By reversing the hooking together of the fingers it emphasizes that the two individuals involved are now enemies. As a variant, little fingers may be used instead of forefingers.

Locality: Widespread.

FOREHEAD KISS

Meaning: Extreme respect.

Action: A subordinate kisses a dominant individual on the forehead.

Background: The kiss of respect is delivered to the forehead, the nose, the hand or the foot of the revered figure. The lower down on the body the kiss is given, the greater the respect that is shown.

Locality: Arab cultures, in formal contexts.
(In all regions it is used informally, between lovers and family members, as an affectionate greeting or passing intimacy.)

FOREHEAD KNOCK

Meaning: Stubborn.

Action: The fist knocks several times on the forehead.

Background: The gesture suggests that the companion is 'thick-skulled' and 'stubborn as a mule'.

Locality: Most used in France, but also observed elsewhere.

FOREHEAD PRESS

Meaning: I feel faint.

Action: The back of the hand is pressed to the forehead. The head is tilted back and the eyes are closed.

Background: This was the melodramatic Victorian swooning gesture, indicating that a woman was about to faint. It is still used today in a mocking context, usually in theatrical circles, as a joke gesture about a companion, saying 'she is behaving like a hysterical prima donna,' or as a camp comment about oneself: 'it is all too much for me'.

Locality: Western world, in theatrical circles.

FOREHEAD RUB

Meaning: A curse on you!

Action: The back of the hand is rubbed on the forehead.

Locality: Jordan.

FOREHEAD SALAAM

Meaning: Respect.

Action: The fingertips are touched briefly to the forehead as the head bows slightly forward. The gesture ends with a forward flourish of the hand.

Background: This is an abbreviated form of the Arab Salaam greeting. In its full version, the hand touches the chest, the mouth and then the forehead. Here, the first two elements are omitted for simplicity, in less formal situations. The essential meaning of the action is 'I offer you my mind'. It is used both as a respectful greeting and as a farewell.

Locality: Arab cultures.

FOREHEAD SCRUB

Meaning: You are foolish.

Action: The closed hand is scrubbed in a circular motion on the forehead.

Background: This is a variation on the 'your brain is going round and round' theme.

Locality: American Indian tribes.

FOREHEAD SLAP

Meaning: How stupid of me!

Action: The palm of the hand strikes the forehead. Usually, the head tilts back slightly at the same time, as if the gesturer is looking up to heaven for guidance.

Background: The gesturer acts out the blow he feels he deserves for being so stupid. Frequently used by someone who has forgotten something important.

Locality: Widespread.

FOREHEAD TAP (1)

Meaning: Crazy!

Action: The forefinger taps the centre of the forehead several times.

Background: Tapping the forehead or the temple is an ambiguous gesture. All it does is to draw attention to the brain by pointing at it. It does not tell us whether the brain in question is clever or stupid. So, in different contexts, the Forehead Tap can mean either 'he is crazy' or 'he is intelligent'. In general, however, the 'crazy' signal is the more common of the two. Where the finger taps the centre of the forehead, as here, the bias is more strongly in favour of the 'crazy' signal.

Locality: Widespread. In Holland, this form of the gesture is exclusively used for signalling 'crazy'.

FOREHEAD TAP (2)

Meaning: Intelligent.

Action: The forefinger taps the forehead several times, usually slightly to one side of the centre line.

Background: This is the alternative message of the gesture. It is most often seen when someone comments about themselves, saying 'I am not so stupid after all', or 'I know what I am doing'.

Locality: Widespread, but most common in Europe and the Americas.

FOREHEAD TAP (3)

Meaning: Crazy!

Action: The fingertips tap the forehead several times.

Background: In this version, the whole hand is used instead of only the forefinger. The tap almost becomes a mild slap, suggesting that the gesturer is annoyed with the person who has done something stupid.

Locality: Widespread, but most common in the Mediterranean region.

FOREHEAD TAP (4)

Meaning: Crazy!

Action: The fingertips of both hands tap the forehead simultaneously, one above each eye.

Background: This is the double-intensity version of Forehead Tap (3), used when the gesturer is particularly exasperated with the stupidity of his companion.

Locality: Widespread, but most common in the Mediterranean region.

FOREHEAD TAP (5)

Meaning: Crazy!

Action: The tips of the forefinger and thumb are placed together and then tapped several times on the centre of the forehead.

Background: This local variant of the gesture has a special origin. The posture of the hand suggests that something minute is being held between the thumb and forefinger, and the inference is that the minute object in question is the companion's brain. The message is: 'You have a brain so small that I could hold it between my thumb and forefinger!'

Locality: Italy, especially the Neapolitan region.

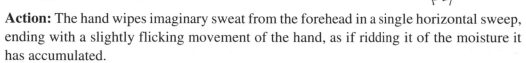

FOREHEAD WIPE

Meaning: Lucky escape.

Action: The hand wipes imaginary sweat from the forehead in a single horizontal sweep, ending with a slightly flicking movement of the hand, as if ridding it of the moisture it has accumulated.

Background: In its primary role, this action does genuinely remove excess sweat from the forehead, preventing it from trickling down into the eyes. This is seen in sporting contests such as tennis matches. In its gestural role, however, the sweat is symbolic and the message is 'I was sweating over that problem but now I am safe.' (It is also used simply as a way of signalling 'how hot I am' or 'this is hot work'.)

Locality: Widespread in the Western world.

FOREHEAD-AND-CHEST SALAAM

Meaning: Respectful greeting.

Action: The fingertips touch the forehead, then the chest, then the forehead again, ending with a flourish of the hand. The gesture is often accompanied by a slight bow.

Background: This is a common variation of the Arab salaam. The basic meaning is 'I give you my mind, my heart, my mind.'

Locality: Arab cultures.

HAIR CLASP

Meaning: How stupid of me!

Action: The hand is brought rapidly up to clasp the top of the head, in a vigorous action.

Background: Self-clasping at moments of alarm is a common human reaction, reflecting the need for self-comfort at times of trouble. The clasp, whether on the top of the head, the forehead, the mouth or the cheek, carries the same, basic, 'relic' message: 'At this moment I need to be clasped protectively, as I was when a child, but now as an adult I must do it for myself.'

Locality: Widespread.

HAIR GROOM

Meaning: I find you attractive.

Action: The hand languorously strokes, lifts, ruffles, swishes or rearranges the hair.

Background: Grooming actions of this kind, favoured especially by long-haired women, are unconscious courting actions.

Locality: Widespread.

HAIR PLUCK

Meaning: The bargain is sealed.

Action: A single hair is plucked from the head.

Background: This is a gesture performed by children when sealing a bargain between them. After the hair is plucked out, it is blown on and the phrase 'Pelillos a la mar' is uttered.

Locality: Spain.

HAIR RAISE

Meaning: Frustration.

Action: A single, long hair is taken between thumb and forefinger and raised up vertically above the head.

Background: This female gesture is a symbolic way of 'tearing your hair out' when feeling intensely frustrated.

Locality: Spain.

HAND BECKON (1)

Meaning: Come here!

Action: The hand makes a sweeping upward movement with the palm up.

Background: This is the typical beckoning action throughout most of Europe. In the very south of the continent, however, this action changes to the palm-down version and this may cause confusion.

Locality: British Isles, Scandinavia, Holland, Belgium, Germany, Austria, France and Yugoslavia.

HAND BECKON (2)

Meaning: Come here!

Action: The hand makes a sweeping downward movement with the palm down.

Background: This is the version of beckoning found around the shores of the Mediterranean. Unfortunately, to more northern Europeans it looks more like a 'go away' or 'go back' sweep of the hand. This error has been known to cause the death of certain individuals who, when approaching a Mediterranean military post, were ordered to 'come here' (for questioning) with the local, palm-down beckon. Assuming that the gesture meant that they must go back, they turned away and were immediately shot as presumed spies trying to make a getaway.

Locality: Spain, Portugal, Italy, Malta, Tunisia, Greece and Turkey.

HAND CHOP (1)

Meaning: I cut through the argument.

Action: One stiff hand chops down on the upturned palm of the other hand.

Background: The speaker mimes the action of cutting downwards with a small axe or chopper (or perhaps imitating a karate chop). The gesture is often used unconsciously during a heated debate, when someone is intent on slicing through the verbal confusion to make a strong, clear point. It is related to the Palm Punch in which the clenched fist is slammed down into the upturned palm, but the chopping action reflects a mood of more precision and slightly less violence than the fist action.

Locality: Worldwide.

HAND CHOP (2)

Meaning: Threat.

Action: The active hand is chopped through the air with repeated, short jerks, but the other hand is not involved in the gesture. The chopping movements are made with a wrist-rotation movement, rather than a downward thrust.

Background: This version of the Hand Chop is made in silence and is usually intended as a threat of 'blows to come' if something is not stopped immediately. It is most often directed at misbehaving children by mildly annoyed adults.

Locality: Italy.

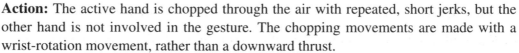

HAND CHOP (3)

Meaning: Threat.

Action: As with Hand Chop (2), but while the chopping action is being made, the thumb holds the forefinger down tightly. The other three fingers are stiffly extended.

Background: This is a curious, hybrid gesture, combining Hand Ring (3) meaning 'Zero' with the threatening Hand Chop (2) gesture. It is sometimes accompanied by the threat 'I will kill you tomorrow', the implication being that 'you are so worthless (such a zero) that I cannot be bothered to kill you today'.

Locality: Most commonly seen in Arab cultures, especially in North Africa, but also occasionally observed in Italy.

HAND CIRCLE (I)

Meaning: Telephone for you.

Action: The hand makes a circling motion near the ear.

Background: This is a relic gesture that mimes the cranking of the handle that was once used to call someone on the telephone. Telephones have long since ceased to use such a handle, but despite this the gesture has survived to the present day in certain regions. In other areas it has been replaced by a gesture that mimes the holding of the more modern apparatus.

Locality: Parts of Europe and the Americas.

HAND CIRCLE (2)

Meaning: Filming.

Action: The hand makes a circling action near the side of the head.

Background: Again, this is a relic action that has long outlived the apparatus on which it is based. It is a mime of an old-fashioned cine-camera that was operated manually by rotating a handle. Because working a modern film camera does not involve any action that is easy to mime, the antique gesture has survived. If someone wishes to signal from a distance that filming is taking place, they still go through the motions of cranking the ancient handle.

Locality: Western world.

HAND CRADLE

Meaning: I don't understand.

Action: One hand is cradled in the other, with both in the palm-up position.

Background: This is the modified Hands Shrug (1). It carries the same 'disclaimer' message as the ordinary shrug – 'I don't know what you mean', 'I can't help you' or 'It is nothing to do with me' – but instead of holding the hands forward, the gesturer keeps them close to the body, in a slightly more defensive position.

Locality: North Africa.

HAND CUP (I)

Meaning: Sexual insult.

Action: The cupped hand mimes the action of lifting something heavy, as if weighing it in the palm. With the fingers grasping the imaginary object, the hand is raised and lowered a short distance. This is done several times.

Background: This gesture is used by one male to insult another. The message is 'what big balls you have'. At first sight this would appear to be a male compliment rather than an insult, but the true meaning of the gesture is 'your balls are heavy because you are incapable of getting a woman to sleep with you'. The gesture is known, in Spanish as 'huevon', which means 'large egg' or 'testicle'.

Locality: Latin America.

HAND CUP (2)

Meaning: I am unhappy.

Action: (As above)

Background: In this version, the gesturer makes a comment, not about his companion, but about himself, saying 'I am unhappy because I have not been able to make love for such a long time.'

Locality: Latin America.

HAND 'DRINK'

Meaning: Drink.

Action: The hand mimes the act of tipping a glass towards the lips, prior to drinking.

Background: This simple mime, understood wherever people drink from glasses, appears to have originated in the British Isles and spread from there around the world. Its message varies slightly according to the context. It can mean: 'I am thirsty', 'Shall we go and have a drink together?', 'Is there anything to drink?' or 'Are you thirsty?' In certain countries where it is popular to drink from a leather bottle, this gesture is replaced by the Thumb-and-Little Finger-Arc, in which the action of tipping up the bottle and squirting a jet of liquid into the mouth is mimed.

Locality: Almost worldwide.

HAND FAN (1)

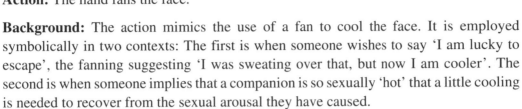

Meaning: I am too hot.

Action: The hand fans the face.

Background: The action mimics the use of a fan to cool the face. It is employed symbolically in two contexts: The first is when someone wishes to say 'I am lucky to escape', the fanning suggesting 'I was sweating over that, but now I am cooler'. The second is when someone implies that a companion is so sexually 'hot' that a little cooling is needed to recover from the sexual arousal they have caused.

Locality: Widespread.

HAND FAN (2)

Meaning: No.

Action: The open right hand, with palm to the left, is moved back and forth in front of the face, as if fanning a flame.

Background: The hand takes over the role of the lateral Head Shake.

Locality: Japan.

HAND FIG (1)

Meaning: Copulation.

Action: The hand is closed and the tip of the thumb is pushed between the first and second finger.

Background: This is the ancient obscene gesture, known as the 'fico', in which the thumb represents the inserted penis.

Locality: In northern Europe the fig sign is given as a bawdy sexual comment: 'This is what I would like to do to you'. In this role it is particularly common in Belgium, Holland, Denmark and Germany. Elsewhere – central France, Greece, Turkey and Corfu – it is much more likely to be employed as a sexual insult: 'Up yours'.

HAND FIG (2)

Meaning: Protection.

Action: (As above)

Background: Like the Hand Horn-Sign (2), this gesture is often used as a defence against the Evil Eye or hostile spirits. For this reason small amulets of hands in the fig posture are still sold as good luck charms. Their superstitious power is based on the idea that any blatant sexual display will distract the evil spirits and divert them from their destructive tasks. This is not always clear to those who wear them, who may be ignorant of their sexual origin.

Locality: Common in Portugal and Brazil. Also found in Sicily.

HAND FIG (3)

Meaning: I've got your nose!

Action: As above, following a pretend grab at a child's nose.

Background: In many countries the gesture is recognized only as part of a child's game in which an adult reaches out to touch the child's nose, then pulls his hand away and shows the child the protruding thumb, saying: 'I've got your nose!'

Locality: Widespread in most of Europe.

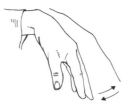

HAND FLAP

Meaning: Leave!

Action: The hand is flapped back and forth as if pushing something away. The force of the 'away' element of the action is stronger than the 'toward' movement.

Background: The hand mimics the dismissive pushing away of some unwanted thing or person. It is the action of an impatient, dominant person who does not care whether he will upset the victim of his gesture. Used seriously it is now rare, but is still common in a joking context.

Locality: Widespread.

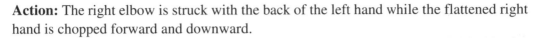

HAND FLICK-DOWN

Meaning: Get lost!

Action: The right elbow is struck with the back of the left hand while the flattened right hand is chopped forward and downward.

Background: The action indicates the direction of the desired departure of the other person. The forceful blow with the left hand suggests the vehemence with which the departure is demanded.

Locality: Holland.

HAND FLICK-UP (1)

Meaning: Get lost!

Action: The right hand is flicked upwards, usually aided in this action by a chopping-down on the right wrist with the left hand.

Background: This has the same meaning as the previous gesture, but uses a slightly different action. The downward chopping movement of the left hand is said to symbolize the severing of a hand of a thief, the message being 'he has been punished like this and sent off to a penal colony.' This forced departure of a thief is thought to be the symbolic basis for the modern 'Get lost!' message.

Locality: Belgium, France, Spain, Italy, Tunisia, Yugoslavia and Greece.

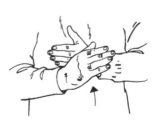

HAND FLICK-UP (2)

Meaning: Departure.

Action: (As above)

Background: Here the gesture is used descriptively instead of as a demand. In place of the 'clear off' and 'go away' signals, it transmits messages such as 'He has gone', 'I am leaving' or 'They have run away'.

Locality: France and Belgium.

HAND FLOP

Meaning: You can't rile me.

Action: The hand is raised and then flopped down towards the companion.

Background: The gesture is essentially an aggressive over-arm blow, but its impact is softened by the fact that it is performed without vigour and with a flat hand. In other words, the message is 'I symbolically hit you over the head for teasing me, but I am not serious so it is only a token blow.'

Locality: Widespread.

HAND FOLD

Meaning: Good.

Action: The hand is held out and the fingers are slowly folded until they meet the thumb, culminating with a 'Hand Purse' position. As this is done the hand is lowered slightly.

Background: This slow-motion hand-closing action is used when someone wishes to pay a compliment. The gesture is sometimes described by its final position rather than by its movement and, for this reason, it is also listed under the heading of Hand Purse (2).

Locality: Corfu, Greece and Turkey.

HAND 'GOITRE'

Meaning: Disbelief.

Action: The hand is cupped below the chin as if holding or describing the shape of a large neck goitre.

Background: In the days when visible physical disabilities were cruelly associated with idiocy, the goitre became a symbol of stupidity, and making the gesture sends the signal that 'What you are saying is so stupid that I do not believe you'.

Locality: South America.

HAND HOLD

Meaning: Friendship.

Action: Two men walk along hand-in-hand.

Background: In western countries, hand-holding between men implies a homosexual relationship. This is not the case in certain regions, where it is considered quite usual for heterosexual, adult male friends to hold hands in public, without the slightest hint of sexuality implied by the action.

Locality: The Middle East, countries around the shores of the Mediterranean, and some parts of Asia.

HAND HORN-SIGN (1) VERTICAL

Meaning: Cuckold.

Action: The hand forms the shape of a horned head by keeping the forefinger and little finger erect, while the thumb holds down the other two fingers.

Background: This is an ancient gesture at least 2500 years old. Because of its antiquity, its true origin is lost, but as many as fourteen different theories have been put forward to explain why making the sign of a horned animal should be considered such a grave insult, suggesting as it does that the victim's wife is unfaithful to him. The most likely explanations are as follows: (1) Irony. The sign says, sarcastically, 'what a great bull you are', meaning the exact opposite. (2) Castration. Many bulls had to be castrated in ancient times to make them docile. The sign says 'you have been symbolically castrated by your wife.' (3) Rage. The suggestion here is that the horn-sign signifies the rage of a mad bull, which is how the husband will behave when he discovers his wife's infidelity. (4) Upstaging. The horns are seen as representing the virility of the wife's lover and their display by the gesturer is a reminder to the victim that his rival has been behaving like a great rutting bull with his wife. Whichever explanation is the true, original one, the fact is that today this gesture can, in certain regions, cause such offence that men have been killed for using it.

Locality: Rare in northern Europe but common in the south and around the shores of the Mediterranean. Particularly common in Spain, Portugal, Italy and Malta.

HAND HORN-SIGN (2) HORIZONTAL

Meaning: Protection from Evil Eye.

Action: The hand makes the horn-sign, as above, but aims it directly at the victim.

Background: Although this version of the horn-sign may sometimes be used with the same meaning as the vertical version – to signal 'cuckold' – it also has a more specific, protective meaning. If someone is thought to be evil or to bring bad luck, the gesturer may protect himself against them by making this sign in their direction. It is an ancient gesture and small models of hands showing it were frequently worn as amulets. These 'lucky charms' are still sold today in certain Mediterranean countries. In this version of the horn-sign, the symbolism is that of the protective bull, or the all-powerful horned god of the ancients. It was this horned god – so protective of them – that became 'converted' into the devil by Christians. So those people still using this sign to defend themselves against evil forces are, in mythological terms, calling upon the devil to come to their aid. For most people today, however, the origins of this gesture have been forgotten and it now has no more significance than 'touching wood' or 'keeping one's fingers crossed', as simple, superstitious devices to bring good luck or avoid bad luck.

Locality: Still used as a protective gesture in most parts of Italy, but only common today on the nearby island of Malta, where it may even be seen as a protective sign painted on boats and motor cars.

HAND HORN-SIGN (3) ROTATE

Meaning: Protection against bad luck.

Action: The hand makes the vertical horn-sign with extended forefinger and little finger and then rotates the hand back and forth several times.

Background: Despite its similarity to the European horn-sign, both in shape and function, this American version appears to have a different origin. It is known as the 'lagarto' or Lizard Gesture and is used by the superstitious to counteract the damage done by someone who has uttered the taboo word 'culebra', or snake.

Locality: South America.

HAND HORN-SIGN (4)

Meaning: Texas University.

Action: The hand makes the horn-sign in any direction.

Background: The Hand Horn-Sign is the gestural emblem of the University of Texas. It is a symbol of the famous longhorn cattle of Texas, and is used by students, especially at sporting events, to support their teams. A visiting Italian team would find it extraordinary to be greeted by massed ranks of their most insulting sign.

Locality: Texas.

HAND JAB

Meaning: I insist.

Action: The hand jabs towards the companion's body, with the fingers all stiffly pointed forward.

Background: When a speaker wishes to impose his ideas in a forceful manner, he may adopt this hand posture and mime the action of jabbing his companion in the chest. Although assertive, this is a less aggressive action than the Forefinger Jab. The solitary forefinger symbolizes a sharper, more damaging stab, while the all-fingers jab represents a blunter and therefore milder assault.

Locality: Worldwide.

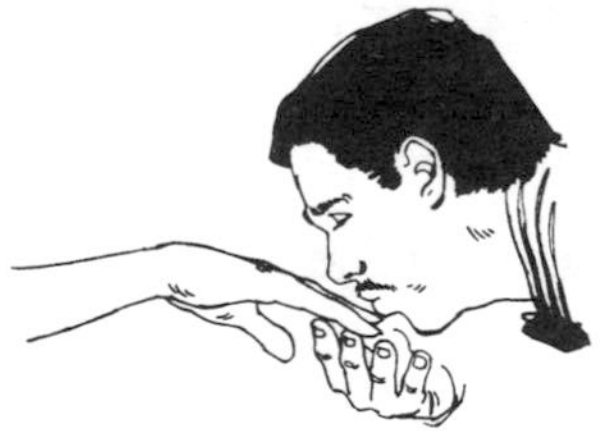

HAND KISS

Meaning: Respectful greeting.

Action: The hand of the companion is gently held while the lips plant a token kiss on the knuckles of or the backs of the fingers. (According to etiquette books, the ideal Hand Kiss should be 'effortless, noiseless and moistureless'.)

Background: This is an antique gesture that only survives in a few special circumstances today. In earlier times, the part of the body kissed was important as a

114

reflection of the relative status of the two individuals involved. Only equals were allowed to kiss one another on the mouth or cheek. Subordinates had to aim lower, and the more subordinate they were, the lower they had to kiss. In extreme cases, where god-like emperors were being greeted, ordinary mortals were only permitted to kiss the dirt at their feet, their shoes, or perhaps the hem of their garment. Slightly less lowly figures were permitted to kiss the knee or the hand. The hand kiss, being the most convenient, was the longest survivor of all these various 'status kisses'. By Victorian times, it was still a common practice to kiss the hand of a lady in greeting or farewell. Today, in most regions, this action is only performed theatrically, with an archly exaggerated flourish, or as a joke. One exception to this is in religious contexts, where a bishop's or an archbishop's ring may be kissed on his gloved hand, as a formal sign of respect by one of the faithful.

Locality: Western world in general, but more likely to be seen in Latin countries.

HAND LOZENGE

Meaning: Vagina.

Action: The hand is displayed with the thumb and forefinger pressed together to create a lozenge-shaped aperture.

Background: This gesture attempts to imitate the shape of the female genitals and is intended either as a hostile sexual insult or as an obscene sexual comment.

Locality: Lebanon and Syria.

HAND MEASURE

Meaning: Any children?

Action: The hand is lowered, with the palm parallel with the floor.

Background: To enquire about children, the gesturer mimes the act of measuring their height with his hand.

Locality: Widespread.

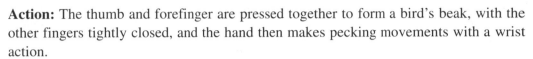

HAND PECK

Meaning: Obscenity.

Action: The thumb and forefinger are pressed together to form a bird's beak, with the other fingers tightly closed, and the hand then makes pecking movements with a wrist action.

Background: Birdlike gestures are often used to parody the precise body movements of male homosexuals.

Locality: Saudi Arabia, Lebanon and Libya.

HAND 'PROW'

Meaning: Apology.

Action: The flat hand is held vertically in front of the face, with the edge of the hand facing forward.

Background: The hand acts like the prow of a ship cutting through water. The action suggests an unfortunate route that must be taken and apologies for the impending intrusion into someone else's space. It is used when the gesturer has to move forward in a way that might be considered impolite, as when crossing someone's path or passing between two people, or being forced to make an unusually close approach for some reason. It is typically accompanied by a slight bow.

Locality: Japan.

HAND PURSE (I)

Meaning: Query.

Action: The fingers are bunched together and the hand is jerked up and down several times with a wrist action.

Background: Essentially this is a request for clarity. It is a 'precision posture' of the hand that says 'I want precise information'. The phrases accompanying it include 'Che

116

vuoi?' or 'Cosa vuoi?', meaning 'What do you want?' and 'Cosa fai?' meaning 'What are you doing?' It may also mean 'What is the matter?', 'What are you saying?' or 'What is it?' It may be used gently as a straight-forward query, but is more commonly seen as an urgent, vigorous action in the context of an irritated or even angry quizzing of a companion. In its most critical form its message is something like 'You fool, why are you doing that?' or simply 'You fool!'

Locality: Italy. This is a remarkably 'national' gesture. It is common throughout Italy but almost totally absent elsewhere. Its use vanishes as one crosses the border into France, Austria or Yugoslavia. (It is, however, seen among Italian expatriates in New York and elsewhere.)

HAND PURSE (2)

Meaning: Good.

Action: The fingertips are bunched together as the hand makes a single downward movement.

Background: In origin this is apparently derived from the Fingertips Kiss, signalling that something is delicious, beautiful or excellent. It differs in omitting the first part of the Fingertips Kiss gesture – the actual lips-touch element. Because of the way this version of the Hand Purse is performed, it can be named by its movement as well as by its final shape. Some see it as a folding of the hand (the movement), others as a folded, or pursed hand (the final position). Because of this, it is also listed under the heading of Hand Fold.

Locality: Corfu, Greece and Turkey.

HAND PURSE (3)

Meaning: Very good! (Sarcastically)

Action: (As above)

Background: In one small location, the Hand Purse gesture takes on a special meaning. It is performed exactly like the 'good' gesture, with a single downward movement of the pursed hand, but instead of signifying that something is excellent it means the precise opposite. For example, if someone tries something and fails, the gesture is given to say, sarcastically, 'Oh, well done!'

Locality: Malta.

HAND PURSE (4)

Meaning: Fear.

Action: The fingertips are bunched together and then opened and closed very slightly.

Background: In this version of the gesture, the opening and closing of the tips of the digits is meant to symbolize the opening and closing of the sphincter muscles that often accompany moments of panic.

Locality: Belgium, France and Portugal.

HAND PURSE (5)

Meaning: Many.

Action: The hand is held in front of the body, with the fingertips bunched together and then opened and closed slightly several times. In an intense form of the gesture, both hands perform the action together. The action is almost identical to the Hand Purse (4) gesture.

Background: In this version the bringing together of the separate digits symbolizes the coming together of a crowd of people. The usual message is 'There are lots of people'.

Locality: Yugoslavia, Spain, the Canary Islands and Spanish South America.

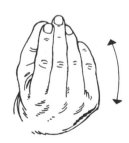

HAND PURSE (6)

Meaning: Be careful.

Action: The pursed hand is raised and lowered very slowly.

Background: In this version of the pursed hand gesture, the slowness of the vertical movement symbolizes the request to 'take care', 'slow down', 'wait', 'be patient'. A common context for its use is on the road, where the driver of one car will ask another not to go so fast by making the gesture out of his car window.

Locality: Tunisia, and other Arab cultures in north Africa and the Middle East.

HAND PURSE (7)

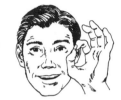

Meaning: I am hungry.

Action: The pursed hand is jerked towards the open mouth several times.

Background: This mimed act of putting food in the mouth is so basic that it is understood the world over.

Locality: Worldwide.

HAND RING (1)

Meaning: O.K., good.

Action: The hand is displayed with the thumb and forefinger tips joined to make a vertical ring.

Background: The ring gesture has been known as a sign of approval since the first century A.D. In origin, it stems from a conversational gesticulation that occurs when a precise point is being made. At such a moment, the speaker often unconsciously brings the tips of the thumb and forefinger together, as if holding some minute object between them. This action automatically forms a ring, and it is from this that the conscious gesture seems to have arisen. Once it was being used, not merely as an accompaniment to speech, but as a deliberate signal in its own right, it came to signify anything that was perfect, excellent or agreeable. In modern times it is generally referred to as the American O.K. Sign, and North America has undoubtedly been the geographical stronghold from which it has spread across the globe, wherever American social influences have been felt. It appears to have failed to gain a foothold, however, in most Arab countries, largely because there are two other versions of the Hand Ring gesture, one threatening and the other obscene.

Locality: Widespread in North America and Europe.

HAND RING (2)

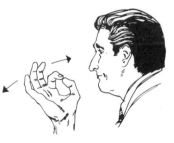

Meaning: Sexual insult.

Action: As above, but the ring may be horizontal instead of vertical.

Background: In this version the ring symbolizes an orifice. Another very old gesture, this can be traced back to ancient Greece, where it appears on certain vase paintings. Although it can refer to either male or female orifices, it is today nearly always used by males about other males. It may either be a friendly comment about the homosexuality of another male, or it may be a sneering insult implying effeminacy.

Locality: Germany, Sardinia, Malta, Tunisia, Greece, Turkey, Russia, the Middle East and parts of South America.

HAND RING (3)

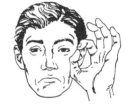

Meaning: Zero.

Action: (As above)

Background: Here the ring formed by the hand symbolizes a nought or a zero, and the implication is that something is 'a big zero', or worthless. This is the precise opposite of the more popular American OK Sign, and leads to confusion where the two meet in the same region.

Locality: Belgium, France and Tunisia.

HAND RING (4)

Meaning: Money.

Action: (As above)

Background: Here the symbolism of the Hand Ring is that of a coin. The gesturer is usually asking for money when using this version of the gesture, but may also be commenting on the high cost of something.

Locality: Japan.

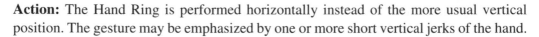

HAND RING (5)

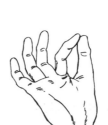

Meaning: Perfection.

Action: The Hand Ring is performed horizontally instead of the more usual vertical position. The gesture may be emphasized by one or more short vertical jerks of the hand.

Background: This is essentially the same gesture as Hand Ring (1), meaning O.K., good, but in this version the meaning is slightly more restricted. When performed in the usual vertical position, the range of meanings includes: OK, good, everything's fine, it is perfect. Here, with the horizontal form of the gesture, the meaning is limited to the last of these: perfection.

Locality: South America.

HAND RING (6)

Meaning: What are you talking about?

Action: This is essentially an inverted Hand Ring gesture. The ring itself is vertical, but the palm faces upward. The hand moves a short distance back and forth, between the gesturer and his companion, several times.

Background: This is similar to the Hand Purse (1) gesture, but performed with only the thumb and forefinger touching. It has the same meaning – questioning, querying what is going on or what is being said.

Locality: Italy.

HAND RING (7)

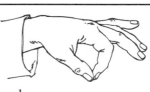

Meaning: Justice.

Action: In this version of the gesture, the ring points downwards.

Background: The hand mimes the action of holding the 'scales of justice' between thumb and forefinger. It is used to say that someone has behaved justly or is a just person.

Locality: Italy.

HAND RING-JERK

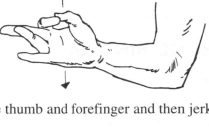

Meaning: Sexual insult.

Action: The hand makes a horizontal ring with the thumb and forefinger and then jerks this ring up and down in the air.

Background: In this version of the Hand Ring gesture, similar to the Fist Jerk, the performer mimes the act of male masturbation. The implied message of the gesture is that the person being insulted is so ineffectual that his only possible form of sexual gratification must be masturbatory. It is a popular taunt employed by fans at football matches when an opposing player has failed in some way.

Locality: Great Britain.

HAND RING-KISS

Meaning: Delicious.

Action: With the hand in the ring position, the tips of the thumb and forefinger are lightly touched to the lips and then the hand is flicked away.

Background: This is the Hand Ring 'perfection' sign combined with a kiss. It carries the same message as the Fingertips Kiss, and is a favourite gesture of chefs when savouring a special dish.

Locality: Continental Europe, especially France.

HAND RING SIDE-PULL (1)

Meaning: Delicious.

Action: The vertical Hand Ring gesture is moved sideways across the front of the gesturer.

Background: The Hand Ring here symbolizes perfection and the sideways movement of the hand emphasizes that perfection.

Locality: Holland.

HAND RING SIDE-PULL (2)

Meaning: She is beautiful!

Action: The horizontal Hand Ring gesture is moved sideways across the front of the gesturer.

Background: The ring gesture symbolizes perfection and the sideways movement of the hand underlines this perfection. (Some individuals use the previous version of this gesture to signify 'beautiful'.)

Locality: Italy, especially in the Neapolitan region.

HAND ROTATE (1)

Meaning: More or less.

Action: The hand rotates back and forth in front of the body.

Background: As the hand tips to left and to right it suggests ambivalence. The gesture is used when asked a question to which the verbal answer would be 'more or less', 'so so' or 'not too bad'.

Locality: Europe and Arab countries.

HAND ROTATE (2)

Meaning: There is something fishy here.

Action: The hand is raised beside the head and rotated back and forth.

Locality: Spain, Germany and Austria.

HAND ROTATE (3)

Meaning: Homosexual.

Action: The hand rotates back and forth in front of the body.

Background: The gesture suggests that someone 'goes either way'.

Locality: Colombia.

HAND SALUTE

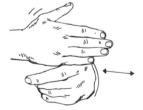

Meaning: Military greeting.

Action: The flat right hand is brought smartly up to the right side of the forehead and then down again.

Background: This is a relic gesture, being the surviving remnant of 'doffing the hat' to a superior. The hand is moved up to the forehead, as an 'intention movement' of grasping the headgear – hat, cap or helmet – but the rest of the action is omitted. In a military context, a subordinate must always salute an officer and the officer must then return the salute. Failure to comply with this rule is an offence. In earlier centuries many gestures were obligatory in this way, but today the Hand Salute is one of the few 'compulsory gestures' remaining in general use. Among non-military personnel it is rarely seen, but occasionally a civilian greeting salute occurs in a light-hearted or joking context.

Locality: Worldwide except in the surviving tribal societies.

HAND SAW

Meaning: Graft.

Action: The edge of one hand makes a sawing motion on the side of the other hand.

Background: This could be called the 'cutting corners' gesture. The action mimes sawing a piece of wood and implies that, in a negotiation or business deal, people are being 'sold short' because of the graft and corruption of those concerned.

Locality: South America.

HAND SCOOP

Meaning: Thief!

Action: The hand scoops downwards through the air.

Background: The gesture mimes the act of a pickpocket scooping away personal possessions.

Locality: Southern Italy.

HAND SCREW

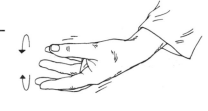

Meaning: Sexual comment.

Action: The hand is held in front of the body and then moved as if unscrewing the lid of an invisible jar.

Background: The gesture, which can best be described as a 'vacuum groping action', is employed as a sexual obscenity. It implies that the gesturer would like to fondle the breasts of the woman in question.

Locality: Lebanon and Syria.

HAND SHAKE (1)

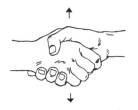

Meaning: Greeting and farewell.

Action: Two companions clasp right hands and then shake them up and down one or more times before breaking the contact.

Background: As a common form of greeting, the Hand Shake is comparatively recent, dating from the early part of the nineteenth century. In earlier centuries, bows, waves, curtseys and flourishes of the hand were the greeting gestures among polite society. The Hand Shake was considered too 'egalitarian'. Today, of course, it fits our modern social attitudes well. If two men meet and one is of much higher rank than the other, they still perform the reciprocal hand shake, in which their actions are identical to one another.

This suits a society in which all men are considered equal but was completely out of place in the highly stratified society of earlier centuries. There remain today certain sexual differences. In some countries women do not offer their hands for shaking while in others they do so. This has led to confusion. Also, in most Islamic countries men who are not closely related to a woman may not touch her in any way, so that if a male visitor politely offers his hand for shaking, his action may be considered an outrage.

Locality: Worldwide in recent years, although in the Middle East, Asia and the Orient, more ancient forms of greeting such as the Salaam, the Namaste, the Wai and the Bow are often still preferred.

HAND SHAKE (2)

Meaning: Congratulation.

Action: (As above)

Background: At the end of a contest, the loser offers his hand to the winner. This is an extension of the everyday greeting Hand Shake because, in effect, the loser is saying to the winner: 'You are no longer the same person – I greet you in your new role.'

Locality: Widespread.

HAND SHAKE (3)

Meaning: Binding a contract.

Action: (As above)

Background: This is the original role of the Hand Shake, before it became a greeting gesture. In medieval times it was employed as a pledge of honour or allegiance, and was usually accompanied by a kneeling position on the part of the subordinate. The clasping of the hands was then more important than the shaking element. We do know that the full Hand Shake occurred as early as the 16th century because in Shakespeare's *As You Like It* there is the phrase: 'they shook hands and swore brothers'.

Locality: European in origin but now widespread.

HAND SHAKE (4)

Meaning: Greeting and farewell.

Action: As above, but with both hands involved. While the right hand is being shaken, the left hand clasps the other side of the shaken hand.

Background: This is the amplified handshake. It has been called the 'Glove Hand Shake', because the two hands cover the other person's hand like a glove, or the 'Politician's Hand Shake' because it is a favourite gesture of public figures who wish to suggest that they are ultra-friendly. It is like a miniature hug, with the companion's hand embraced as intimately as possible. The effect is to give a powerful friendship signal while at the same time retaining the formality of this type of greeting.

Locality: Widespread in diplomatic, political and business circles.

HAND SHAKE (5)

Meaning: Greeting and farewell.

Action: As above, but with the left hand grasping the arm of the companion.

Background: This is a further amplification of the normal Hand Shake. The hand that is clasping the arm is performing a partial embrace. The message is 'I am formally shaking hands with you, but I feel such a strong bond of friendship that I could almost hug you.' In other words, this is a hybrid gesture, halfway between a Hand Shake and an embrace. When the greeting is stronger still, the Hand Shake is abandoned altogether and both parties embrace fully.

Locality: Widespread in diplomatic, political and business circles.

HAND SHAKE (6)

Meaning: Greeting and farewell.

Action: This is a normal Hand Shake except that the initiator of the greeting offers his hand in a palm-down position. This forces the companion to respond with a palm-up position.

Background: This is the Hand Shake of a dominant person who wishes to 'gain the upper hand'. By offering his hand in the palm-down position, he presents a challenge to his companion. Either the hand posture is accepted, in which case the egalitarian quality of the greeting is lost, or he has to make an issue of it by refusing to cooperate. In ordinary Hand Shakes, both people involved perform identical actions – each with a 'thumb-above' hand position – regardless of their relative status. But in the Palm-Down Hand Shake, the initiator rejects this and expresses his high status in a subtle way.

Locality: Widespread in diplomatic, political and business circles.

HAND SLAP (1)

Meaning: I have made a stupid mistake.

Action: The left hand is held limply in front of the body and its back is slapped with the right hand.

Background: The gesture mimes the action of being slapped by a parent or schoolteacher and indicates self-punishment.

Locality: Britain.

HAND SLAP (2)

Meaning: I have contempt for you.

Action: With the palm of the left hand held to the front, its back is slapped by the right hand.

Background: The action mimics a parent slapping the hand of a naughty child. In this way it demeans the adult to whom the gesture is made.

Locality: Saudi Arabia.

HAND SWEEP

Meaning: Thief.

Action: The hand sweeps across the top of a table, as if gathering up something.

Background: The gesture mimes the action of hurriedly scooping up money that has been left lying on the table. In some regions this means 'there is a thief about', but in others it simply signals 'money' or, more specifically, 'pay up!'

Locality: South America, where it generally signals that 'someone is stealing', except in Peru, where it is more likely to mean simply 'money'.

HAND SWIVEL

Meaning: He is crazy!

Action: The fingertips of one hand are placed under the elbow of the other arm, the forearm of which is held vertically. The upper hand then swivels back and forth like a rotating handle.

Background: This gesture is known as the 'Pepper' and is said to mimic a pepper-grinder, the idea being that the person referred to as crazy has a brain that is madly grinding away, instead of being calm and sensible.

Locality: Southern Italy.

HAND THRUST

Meaning: She is a prostitute.

Action: The flat hand, palm down, makes thrusting movements back and forth in front of the body.

Background: Like many sexual gestures, this one imitates the thrusting movements of copulation.

Locality: South America.

HAND TOSS

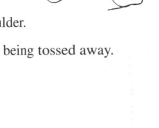

Meaning: He can get lost!

Action: The hand throws an imaginary object over the shoulder.

Background: The gesture symbolizes something worthless being tossed away.

Locality: France.

HAND TURN

Meaning: Insult.

Action: Held at waist level, the hand is quickly turned over by a single rotation.

Background: The movement mimes the action of tipping something over and down on to the ground, the implication being that it is worthless and only fit to be thrown away.

Locality: Lebanon and Syria.

HAND V-SIGN (1)

Meaning: Victory.

Action: The first two fingers make a V-sign. The palm faces forwards.

Background: For once, we know the exact date on which a gesture was created. The V-for-Victory sign was invented on January 14th 1941 by a Belgian lawyer with the appropriate name of Victor De Lavelaye. In a wartime broadcast he proposed the V-sign as the symbol for a propaganda campaign against the Nazis. Winston Churchill took up the idea and began to use the sign publicly. Even after the war, he continued to employ it as a personal emblem and it gradually came to stand for any kind of victory – military, political, sporting or individual.

Locality: From its British origins it has now spread to become almost worldwide.

HAND V-SIGN (2)

Meaning: Insult.

Action: The first two fingers make a V-sign. The palm faces backwards.

Background: This uniquely British insult puzzles foreigners, who confuse it with the V-for-Victory sign. For them, a V-sign means Victory regardless of the position of the hand, but for the British the direction of the palm is crucial. When the palm faces the body of the gesturer, the Victory symbolism is over-ruled by the insult message. But what is the symbolism of the rude V-sign? This has mystified even the British. When they were asked to explain the significance of the gesture they gave no fewer than ten different explanations. The most plausible of these were:

1. A badly made cuckold sign. The well-known cuckold horn-sign is made by extending the forefinger and the little finger. A slight modification, due perhaps to ignorance, would convert this into the V-sign, using the second finger in place of the little finger.

2. An enlarged phallus sign. The obscene middle-finger sign, dating from ancient Rome, employs a single finger as a phallic symbol. By using two, the V-sign is thought to symbolize an enlarged, and therefore 'improved' phallus, making it more threateningly obscene.

3. A female genital sign. This interpretation sees the two fingers as representing either the female pubic triangle, or the open female genitals, or the spread female legs.

4. Inserted fingers sign. Some gesturers believe that they are miming the action of inserting male fingers during sexual foreplay.

All these, and other explanations have been given by people who employ the V-sign as a gross insult. In all cases they are merely guessing at the origin of the sign, but this is of little consequence. For them the gesture carries an intensely insulting signal and the fact that they are understanding it in different ways does nothing to lessen its impact. In addition to these modern sexual explanations, there is one quite different, historical explanation that may reveal how the gesture first came into being. It is said that, during the Norman invasion, English archers were warned that, when they lost their battles, they would have their bow-fingers (the first and second fingers) amputated, to make it impossible for them ever to fire their arrows at the French again. They dreaded this punishment, which would destroy their military skills for life, and were so relieved when they won a famous battle that, afterwards, they all taunted the defeated Frenchmen by holding up their first and second fingers to show that they were still there. If this was the true origin of the insult V-sign, it would explain the uniquely British occurrence of the gesture. With this small piece of history forgotten, the gesture would later be explained by a variety of modern rationalizations.

Locality: Almost entirely confined to the British Isles. It is only found elsewhere in ex-colonies of the British Empire where the British influence has been particularly strong, as in the case of the island of Malta.

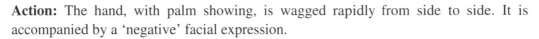

HAND WAG

Meaning: No!

Action: The hand, with palm showing, is wagged rapidly from side to side. It is accompanied by a 'negative' facial expression.

Background: Here, a hand movement is being used as a substitute for the negative Head Shake. It is most often used as a long-distance signal – in a restaurant, an office, or at a party – when the ordinary Head Shake for 'No thanks!' might not be clearly seen.

Locality: Widespread.

HAND WAVE (I)

Meaning: Hallo, goodbye or help.

Action: With the palm showing, the raised hand is waved from side to side.

Background: This is the common, worldwide method of waving, understood everywhere. In origin, it is simply the easiest way of making oneself visible from a distance. For this reason it is also used as a way of getting attention when in distress. Because of its double message – greeting and distress – it can be confusing and in certain contexts alternatives have been devised to signal distress. At sea, for example, anyone in difficulties is supposed to raise and lower sideways their outstretched arms. If their boat is stranded, for example, this will ensure that passing vessels do not imagine that a simple, friendly greeting is being given. Unfortunately, those not familiar with the marine code may be so puzzled by the arms being raised and lowered, that they simply ignore the signal.

Locality: Common almost everywhere, but less so in Italy.

HAND WAVE (2)

Meaning: Hallo or goodbye.

Action: With the palm showing, the hand is flapped up and down.

Background: This is a common variant of the Hand Wave. It is mostly employed when adults are waving to children, or by children themselves. It is easily confused with the palm-down Hand Beckon.

Locality: Common almost everywhere, but less so in Italy.

HAND WAVE (3)

Meaning: Hallo or goodbye.

Action: The hand is waved in the air but the palm is hidden from the companion. The movement of the hand is similar to the one used when embracing someone or patting them on the back.

Background: This is the 'Italian Wave' and has a different origin, being derived from the act of hugging a companion and patting them on the back. The person waving in this way is performing a 'vacuum embrace'. In ordinary usage, the movements are usually fast, but a slowed down version is employed by the Pope when waving from his balcony. He uses the wave to symbolically embrace his flock.

Locality: Italy, including Sicily and Sardinia. Outside Italian territories it is rare, but may be seen in certain special contexts, such as the British Royal Wave on ceremonial occasions.

HAND 'WRITE'

Meaning: Please bring me the bill.

Action: The hand is held up towards a waiter and then mimes the act of writing.

Background: Across a noisy, busy restaurant, this gesture, at the end of a meal, is not considered rude because it saves the waiter the trouble of making his way across the room to find out what the diner wants.

Locality: Common throughout the Western world.

HANDS CLASP

Meaning: Pleading.

Action: The hands are clasped in front of the chest with the fingers interlocked.

Background: This is a modified posture of prayer, used both for formal praying and for personal pleading.

Locality: Italy.

HANDS CLASP-RAISE

Meaning: Greeting.

Action: The right hands are clasped, as in the ordinary Hand Shake, but then, while still clasped, they are raised high in the air. At the top of the movement, they are disengaged.

Background: This is a local variant of the widespread Hand Shake greeting.

Locality: Africa – especially with the Bantu.

HANDS CROSS

Meaning: No.

Action: The hands are moved back and forth across one another, with the palms showing.

Background: This is the two-handed version of the Hand Waggle, using arm movement in place of wrist movement. It is most often employed as a 'No more, thank you' signal.

Locality: Widespread.

HANDS 'DONKEY' (1)

Meaning: He is an ass.

Action: The hands are held together, palm to palm, with the thumbs erect and the little fingers separated.

Background: This gesture mimes the head of a donkey and suggests that someone is a 'stupid ass'.

Locality: Italy.

HANDS 'DONKEY' (2)

Meaning: He is an ass.

Action: The flat hands are placed one on top of the other and the thumbs are projected sideways.

Background: The hands form a crude mimic of a donkey's head, with the thumbs as the ears. As with the previous gesture, this implies that someone is a 'stupid ass'.

Locality: Italy.

HANDS 'FLUTE'

Meaning: I am bored.

Action: The hands mime the action of playing a flute.

Background: The implication is that the words being spoken have about as much meaning as the endless tootling of a flute.

Locality: France.

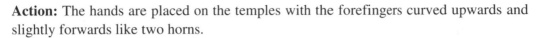

HANDS HORN-SIGN (1)

Meaning: Cuckold.

Action: The hands are placed on the temples with the forefingers curved upwards and slightly forwards like two horns.

Background: This is the two handed version of the Vertical Hand Horn-Sign, and is occasionally used instead of the typical one-handed form.

Locality: Mediterranean region.

HANDS HORN-SIGN (2)

Meaning: Jealous.

Action: (As above)

Background: The horn-sign that means 'cuckold' in the West, signals 'jealousy' in the East. A Japanese bride wears a special headgear called a 'horn-hider' at her wedding, to cancel her feelings of jealousy during the ceremony.

Locality: Japan.

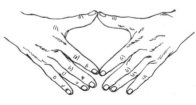

HANDS 'LOZENGE'

Meaning: Prostitute.

Action: The hands are pressed together to form a lozenge or diamond-shaped aperture between them.

Background: This gesture delineates the shape of the female genitals and is used in connection with overt sexual encounters. Its most common use is for one man to signal to another, concerning a woman, that 'she is a prostitute'.

Locality: South America.

HANDS 'ORIFICE'

Meaning: Sexual insult.

Action: The hands form the two halves of a large circle.

Background: This is an obscene anal gesture the message of which is 'I will give you an orifice this large'.

Locality: The Neapolitan region of Italy.

HANDS PRAY-SHAKE

Meaning: What do you want from me?

Action: The fingertips are brought together, as if in a posture of prayer, but then the hands are shaken up and down urgently several times. They are moved vertically from the wrist, in an arc.

Background: This can best be described as an 'irritated pleading'. It is a hybrid gesture, combining an act of praying with wringing the hands. The prayer element says 'What in God's name do you want from me?' and the hand-wringing says: 'I implore you'.

Locality: Italy.

HANDS RAISE-CLASP

Meaning: Victory!

Action: The hands are raised above the head and as they make the upward movement they are clasped tightly together. Once they reach their highest point they may be held still there for several seconds, or they may be jerked back and forth, before being lowered again.

Background: This gesture began as a boxer's triumph display and has since spread to other sports and even to non-sporting occasions. Its impact is based on the fact that it makes the gesturer seem 'taller', as do almost all triumph displays. In the case of boxing it is also a demonstration that the fighter concerned is still capable of holding his arms high in the air, despite the punishment he has received from his opponent. In addition, it has the benefit of being highly visible to the crowds watching, even if, in the crush, they are unable to see the rest of the boxer's body.

Locality: Initially in the United States, but now widespread.

HANDS ROLL

Meaning: There are complications.

Action: The hands roll around one another in a circular motion.

Background: The movement of the hands represents an on-going process that seems never-ending.

Locality: South America.

HANDS SCISSOR

Meaning: That is finished!

Action: The hands are crossed over one another and then forcibly sliced apart, as if they are the blades of a large pair of scissors.

Background: When a speaker wishes to finish an argument – 'I am sorry, but that is all I have to say on the matter' – he may mime the action of a pair of shears or large scissors, symbolically snipping off the debate. This action is frequently performed unconsciously during the heat of the moment.

Locality: Worldwide.

HANDS SHRUG (1)

Meaning: Disclaimer.

Action: The hands are shrugged in response to a question. The posture of the hands is palm-up, with a slight curl of the fingers. The degree of this curling increases from the forefinger to the little finger.

Background: The name 'bowling posture' has been used in an attempt to describe the

138

shape of the Hands Shrug, because it is similar to the hand position employed when grasping a large bowling ball.

Locality: Widespread, but essentially a Western gesture. It is so common in the West that most people imagine it to be a universal gesture. This is not so. For example, a recent report states that, thanks to international influence 'some Japanese are now beginning to shrug'.

HANDS SHRUG (2)

Meaning: Deception.

Action: The hands are shrugged while the gesturer is speaking. (His verbal comments do not involve a disclaimer.)

Background: When a speaker is making a disclaimer, he may perform the Hands Shrug and the gesture then supports his statement. But if he unconsciously performs the gesture when he is not making a disclaimer, then it may indicate that he is lying.

Locality: (As above)

HANDS 'THROTTLE'

Meaning: I could throttle you!

Action: The hands mime the action of choking someone to death.

Background: This is a two-handed version of the Throat Grasp (1) gesture. Instead of grasping his own throat the gesturer employs both hands to squeeze an imaginary neck in front of him.

Locality: Widespread.

HANDS T-SIGN (1)

Meaning: Time-out.

Action: One hand is held horizontally while the other touches it vertically from underneath.

Background: This gesture, which is a simple mime of the letter T, originated in American Football, but has now spread to other contexts. It is used socially when one person wants to signal to a companion that the moment has come to take a break in whatever is happening.

Locality: Originally only in the United States but now spreading.

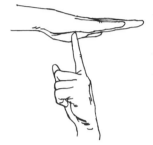

HANDS T-SIGN (2)

Meaning: (As above)

Action: In this version the lower hand uses only the forefinger to make the vertical element of the letter T.

Background: This version of the gesture, which has been called the 'Umbrella Gesture', is employed in a working context. At the end of the day, it is used to signal to a group of workmen that 'it is time to stop work and lie down'. It may be a local variation on the North American 'Time-out' signal, or it may have arisen independently, with the horizontal hand symbolizing the reclining bodies of the workmen after they have stopped work.

Locality: Peru.

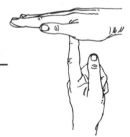

HANDS T-SIGN (3)

Meaning: Invitation to join in.

Action: Exactly as in Hands T-Sign (2) above, with only the forefinger making the vertical element.

Background: This gesture is used to call friends together, usually for a game or some other group activity.

Locality: Italy.

HANDS WRING

Meaning: Please help me.

Action: The tightly clamped hands are jerked back and forth in front of the body.

Background: This is the ancient gesture asking for mercy. Today it is seen in religious contexts when someone is begging for God's help, or in dramatic social encounters, where one person is pleading with another. In origin it is a mimed hug, with the arms performing the action, as it were, in thin air, rather than around the body of another person.

Locality: Worldwide.

HAT RAISE

Meaning: Greeting.

Action: The right hand removes the hat from the head briefly, then replaces it.

Background: This form of greeting has a long and complex history. In earlier centuries, whole chapters were written in etiquette books concerning the most minute details of how to 'doff the hat' correctly. This varied from epoch to epoch. In medieval times, the hat was removed as part of the general body-lowering process, when an inferior encountered a superior. Two elements were involved in the origin of the gesture. The hat was removed (1) because it was impolite to conceal the identity of the person performing the greeting (many early hats and hoods covered much of the head) and (2) because the wearing of a hat increased the height of the human figure and therefore, in order to lower the body in front of a dominant individual, the removal of the hat was the first action to take. In medieval times, the hat, once removed, was held in the hands until the encounter was at an end. It was considered important not to hold it in such a way that would allow the dominant individual to see inside it. This was because it was supposed that the inside would be dirty and this would offend the sensibilities of the dominant one. This rule was changed in the eighteenth century, when it became fashionable for men to wear wigs. It was then specifically required that the doffed hat be held in such a way that the inside was clearly visible – the idea being to demonstrate that it was now definitely not dirty. All this hat-doffing was done with great flourishes and deep bows, but the tradition gradually declined in the nineteenth century and the gesture ended up as a mere removal of the hat and then its quick replacement. Later still, in the twentieth century, the removal became little more than a slight lift of the hat from the head and then an instant replacement.

Locality: Western world. In the East, the removal of the hat is largely replaced by the removal of the shoes as an 'introductory courtesy'.

HAT TIP

Meaning: Greeting.

Action: The hand rises to briefly touch the brim of the hat.

Background: This is the ultimate reduction of the ancient Hat Removal gesture. 'Tipping' the hat is today frequently all that is left of this greeting ritual, the fingers merely touching or momentarily grasping the brim of the hat before being lowered again.

Locality: (As above).

HEAD BECKON

Meaning: Come here!

Action: The head is jerked backwards.

Background: This is today an arrogant way of summoning someone to come closer, employed only by dominant individuals with no thought for the feelings of the other person involved. What makes this form of beckoning appear rude is the idea, inherent in the gesture, that the summoned person is of so little worth that the dominant individual cannot even be bothered to expend the effort of raising a hand, to beckon in the more customary manner. One context in which this does not apply is the 'secretive beckon', when the Hand Beckon would be too conspicuous and the Head Beckon is being used covertly, for the eyes of one person only.

Locality: Widespread.

HEAD CLAMP

Meaning: Superiority.

Action: The body leans back, with the hands clamped firmly at the back of the head.

Background: This display reveals that someone feels no need to show eagerness or attention. Instead of leaning forward eagerly, he adopts the opposite posture. His hands act like a pillow supporting his head. In a business context, this gives him the aggressively relaxed appearance of someone who feels smug and completely in charge of the situation.

Locality: Most common in North America, especially the South-west, but seen elsewhere.

HEAD NOD

Meaning: Yes!

Action: The head is moved up and down vertically one or more times, with the up elements and the down elements of equal strength, or with the down elements slightly stronger.

Background: It has been suggested that this action originates from the downward movement of the baby's head when it is accepting the breast. Others see it as an abbreviated form of submissive body-lowering – in other words, as a miniature bow.

Locality: Worldwide.

HEAD PAT

Meaning: Friendly greeting for small child.

Action: An adult gently pats a child on the top of the head.

Background: This common gesture is of interest because in certain parts of the world it is deeply offensive. In the West, parents or friendly adults frequently pat a child on the head as a substitute for a greeting such as the hand-shake, which seems inappropriate when children are very young. Unfortunately, in certain Far East countries, the top of the head must never be touched in this way, even in the case of small children, because the head is considered the most sacred part of the body and touching it is seen as an offence against the deity.

Locality: Widespread except in the Far East. Especially taboo in Thailand.

HEAD ROLL (I)

Meaning: Maybe yes, maybe no.

Action: The head is tilted left and right alternately.

Background: This is a gesture expressing doubt or indecision. By moving first one way and then the other, the head movement symbolizes the ambivalence of the mood. It asks the question 'should I lean this way or that way?' Many people demonstrate the same ambivalence by tilting the hand side to side in a similar movement.

Locality: This is thought of as primarily a Jewish gesture, but it is well known all over eastern and central Europe and is understood almost everywhere, even by people who do not perform it themselves.

HEAD ROLL (2)

Meaning: Yes!

Action: (As above)

Background: In a few cultures the Head Roll, or 'Head Wobble' as it is sometimes called, signifies an affirmative. It is used instead of the much more familiar Head Nod. This can cause great confusion, because it looks so similar to the Head Shake. Foreigners often think that a 'Head Wobbler' is saying 'No!', when in reality he is saying 'Yes'. Eventually, they learn the local gesture and then start to use it when they want to say 'Yes!' Unfortunately the local inhabitants do not always know whether their visitors have switched to their Yes/No code, and imagine that they are still using the foreign 'No!' Misunderstandings are endless.

Locality: Bulgaria, India and Pakistan. This gesture has a strange distribution, with no obvious link between the European Bulgarians and the Asiatics. Some observers claim to have witnessed its occasional use in parts of Greece, Turkey and Iran, which would suggest an ancient 'gestural corridor' between Eastern Europe and central Asia.

HEAD SCRATCH

Meaning: Puzzled.

Action: The hand scratches the hair on top of the head.

Background: Scratching occurs as a natural reaction to conflict. When performed deliberately, this gesture is a stylized version of this automatic response.

Locality: Widespread.

HEAD SHAKE

Meaning: No!

Action: The head is turned from side to side, with equal emphasis left and right.

Background: This action originates as a juvenile food-refusal movement. When a baby does not want food, either at the breast or when being spoon-fed, it twists its head away sideways. This movement therefore becomes associated with a negative response.

Locality: Widespread.

HEAD SIDE-TURN

Meaning: No!

Action: The head is turned sharply to one side and then back to its central position again.

Background: This is a local variant of the more usual Head Shake negative.

Locality: Ethiopia.

HEAD SLAP

Meaning: How stupid of me!

Action: The hand is brought rapidly up to strike the side of the head, in a vigorous action.

Background: The hand mimes the action of someone else slapping the gesturer's head, for being so stupid.

Locality: Widespread, but most commonly used in central and eastern Europe.

HEAD SUPPORT

Meaning: Boredom.

Action: The weight of the head is supported by the hand.

Background: Although this gesture is sometimes said to indicate 'thoughtfulness', its underlying message is that the person concerned is bored with the proceedings. Because it is not a deliberate or stylized action and is performed almost unconsciously, it is a useful indicator to a speaker about the mood of his audience.

Locality: Worldwide.

HEAD TAP

Meaning: I am fed up to here.

Action: The flat hand is placed horizontally on top of the head, where it taps the crown several times.

Background: This is a more extreme version of the 'fed up to here' gesture, outdoing the more usual Chin Tap by going even further up, to the highest point of the human body.

Locality: South America.

HEAD TOSS (I)

Meaning: No!

Action: The head is tilted vigorously backwards.

Background: Most people, throughout the world, shake the head from side to side when saying 'No!', but in a few regions there is an alternative head movement, the Head Toss. Both appear to have originated from a childhood action. When an infant has had enough to eat, but the parent insists in trying to push one more spoonful into its mouth, one of two reactions may occur. The child may either twist the head sideways, or tilt it upwards, in an attempt to reject the food offering. In other words, moving the head smartly sideways or upwards means 'No!' for the infant. The sideways head movement has developed into the familiar, negative Head Shake in most cultures, but in a few cases it is the other action, the upward tilt of the head, that has became the negative Head Toss.

Locality: This action has been observed in most Arab cultures. In Europe it is usually known as the 'Greek No' and has spread from there to modern-day Turkey, Corfu, Malta, Sicily and the southern parts of Italy. Of particular interest is the fact that, in Italy, its use only extends as far north as the Massico range of mountains between Naples and Rome. This is the point at which the Greek colonization of Italy stopped two and a half thousand years ago. This 'gesture barrier' reveals that ancient forms of body language can be extremely conservative and show little change over the centuries, despite the mobility of modern living.

HEAD TOSS (2)

Meaning: Yes!

Action: (As above)

Background: In certain regions this gesture means the exact opposite, signalling an affirmative. The origin is different here, this Head Toss being derived from the backward tilt of the head that often accompanies a greeting of a friend.

Locality: Ethiopia.

HEART CLASP (I)

Meaning: I love you.

Action: The palm of the right hand is clasped to the left side of the chest, covering the heart.

Background: In more romantic times, this was the lover's gesture when declaring undying love. The symbolic message of the gesture is 'you are so beautiful that you make my heart beat faster.' In most countries today it is only used in this way in playful contexts, but it does live on as a genuine, spontaneous gesture in certain South American countries.

Locality: Widespread.

HEART CLASP (2)

Meaning: Loyalty.

Action: (As above)

Background: This is an ancient gesture with which to demonstrate one's loyalty, or to swear an oath of allegiance. Symbolically it says 'my heart is yours.' It is known from Classical Greece where, for slaves, it was a gesture of obedience, signifying that they were awaiting the command of their master. Today it is most frequently seen on great public occasions, especially political or sporting, when men are offering devotion to their flag, usually during the playing of their National Anthem. In military contexts it is also employed by senior civilians. There it acts as a substitute for the typical hand-to-forehead salute of the uniformed personnel. In earlier decades, when the formal wear of statesmen included headgear, the hat was removed from the head and held over the heart. Now the hand makes the same movement, even though hatless.

Locality: Most commonly observed today in the United States of America.

HEART CROSS

Meaning: I am telling the truth.

Action: The forefinger of the right hand traces a cross on the chest, over the position of the heart.

Background: The gesture is sometimes made silently but is usually accompanied by the phrase 'Cross my heart and hope to die'. To a devout Christian this is seen as a sacred, symbolic gesture that makes the sign of the cross on the heart, with the message 'may God strike me down if I am telling a lie.' The gesture survives among modern non-Christians because the act of crossing the heart can also be taken as a symbolic quartering of the heart, as a punishment for the liar.

Locality: Widespread in Christian countries.

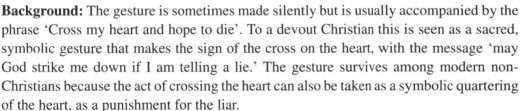

HEART PAT

Meaning: I need help.

Action: The palm of the right hand pats the chest in the region of the heart.

Background: The action mimes a fast heartbeat, implying that the gesturer is in a state of panic.

Locality: Most common in the Middle East.

HEART PRESS

Meaning: Deep respect.

Action: The left fist is covered by the right hand and both are then pressed against the heart.

Background: This action of hugging the heart for someone is a sign of great respect, usually shown towards the elderly.

Locality: Taiwan.

HEELS CLICK

Meaning: Respectful greeting.

Action: The heels are audibly clicked as the legs are brought sharply together. A brief head bow often accompanies the action.

Background: In origin this is a military action – part of the 'coming to attention' when an officer approaches. In civilian life it retains the military quality, but may be used as a formal, respectful greeting.

Locality: In its non-military role this action is confined largely to Germany, Austria and certain South American countries such as Argentina.

HIPS JERK

Meaning: Sexual obscenity.

Action: The hips are thrust forward repeatedly while the elbows are held to the sides. The forearms are bent forward, and may be jerked backwards as the hips move forward.

Background: The action mimes the pelvic thrusts of the male during copulation. The arms are positioned as if holding a female body.

Locality: Widespread.

KNEE KNEEL

Meaning: Formal subordination.

Action: The body is lowered so that one knee is resting on the ground.

Background: In medieval times, when the full kneel was reserved exclusively for submission to God, the 'half-kneel' became the traditional gesture for a subordinate to make towards a dominant individual. As the centuries passed it became increasingly rare. It was gradually replaced by the curtsey and the bow, until these too were largely overtaken by the modern, egalitarian Hand Shake. In Victorian times it was still used by young males at the moment of proposing marriage. Today the one-knee kneel is observed on only the most formal occasions, such as the receiving of a knighthood from the monarch.

Locality: Europe, rare.

KNEE SCRATCH

Meaning: Good luck.

Action: The hand is lowered to scratch one knee.

Background: This is a superstitious action meant to bring good luck or avoid bad luck. In particular it is thought to increase the chances of finding a husband in the near future. It is performed by girls in country districts whenever they see 'three priests or three negroes', and may cause some annoyance to the trio who have provoked it.

Locality: South America.

KNEES CLASP

Meaning: I am about to leave.

Action: The seated figure leans forward and clasps both knees with the hands.

Background: This is the 'intention movement' of rising from the seated position and is used as a signal (either consciously or unconsciously) that someone is becoming impatient to depart.

Locality: Worldwide.

KNEES KNEEL

Meaning: Formal subordination.

Action: The body is lowered so that both knees are resting on the ground.

Background: In ancient times, subordinates sank to the ground on both knees when confronting an overlord, a king, or any other dominant figure, but by the medieval period this had changed. From that time onwards men were instructed to offer only one knee to their rulers and to reserve the full kneel exclusively for God. Today, in the Western world, this distinction is still observed, with the two-knee kneel being performed only by worshippers in church and by those giving thanks to God, such as sportsmen following a moment of great triumph.

Locality: Widespread.

KNUCKLE KISS

Meaning: Gratitude.

Action: The gesturer kisses the knuckles of the right hand, then rotates the hand so that the palm is facing upwards. At the same time the eyes are raised to heaven.

Background: The action offers a kiss of thanks to the deity above.

Locality: Arab cultures.

KNUCKLE RUB

Meaning: Sexual interest.

Action: When a man shakes hands with an attractive woman, he rubs her knuckles gently back and forth with his thumb.

Background: Rhythmic movements of the 'phallic' thumb often carry sexual messages.

Locality: Middle East.

KNUCKLE STRIKE

Meaning: I dare you!

Action: The knuckles of one fist are struck with the other fist.

Locality: Turkey.

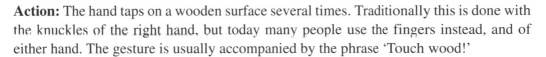

KNUCKLE TOUCH-WOOD

Meaning: Protection.

Action: The hand taps on a wooden surface several times. Traditionally this is done with the knuckles of the right hand, but today many people use the fingers instead, and of either hand. The gesture is usually accompanied by the phrase 'Touch wood!'

Background: This is an ancient superstitious practice dating back to the days of tree-worship, when it was the custom to touch the sacred oak to placate the powerful Tree Spirits. The roots of the mighty oak were thought to descend into the underworld. (Later, Christians converted this pagan practice into 'touching Christ's cross for protection'.) Today, for most people, any kind of wood is used and in any condition, but more natural wood, especially oak, is still preferred by those who take such beliefs seriously. The gesture is made to prevent punishment for boasting. This is because it was thought that evil spirits would be attracted by any mention of good fortune. If they detected anyone commenting on how lucky they had been, they would be jealous and would immediately try to destroy that good luck. An old proverb summed it up by saying: 'He who talks of happiness summons grief'. Even today, in our largely rational, post-superstitious world, many people still experience a moment of slight panic when they say something like 'I have never had a puncture in this car', and then search frantically for some piece of wood among the plastic and metal, to protect themselves from having 'tempted fate'. Winston Churchill was quoted as saying 'I rarely like to be any considerable distance from a piece of wood.'.

Locality: Widespread, but especially common in the British Isles. In Holland, the underside of a wooden table must be touched because there the wood is unpolished and in a more natural state. In some regions, metal is touched instead of wood, because metal was once a precious and therefore a 'magical' substance.

152

LEG CLAMP

Meaning: Stubborn.

Action: The crossed leg is clamped firmly into position by the hands.

Background: This is the unconscious reaction of someone who is resisting persuasion in a discussion. The gesture says 'My ideas, like my body, are clamped firmly in position and will not budge an inch'.

Locality: Widespread.

LEG STROKE

Meaning: I find you attractive.

Action: The companion absent-mindedly strokes their own leg.

Background: When people find their companions attractive, they may unconsciously do to their own bodies what they would like their companions to do to them. For example, young girls at pop concerts hug themselves as they would like to be hugged by their idols. In ordinary social encounters such extreme reactions are rare, but telltale signs still exist. A casual stroking of the body while listening to a companion, or while talking to them, indicates a desire to be caressed by them, regardless of what statements are being made at the time. Leg stroking is the most common form of this reaction.

Locality: Widespread.

LEGS CROSS (I) ANKLE-ANKLE

Meaning: I am politely relaxed.

Action: With the figure seated, the legs are crossed at the ankles.

Background: The act of crossing the legs suggests relaxation because the posture makes it difficult to spring into action suddenly if required. An attentive subordinate sits forward, with legs uncrossed. Someone who is more at ease, or more dominant, can afford to be in a state of less 'readiness'. The ankle-ankle cross is the least extreme form of leg crossing and is therefore the most polite, or demure. It is the posture usually adopted by the sitting figures in a formal group photograph. The Queen, for example, is never seen in public with any other form of leg-crossing.

Locality: Worldwide.

LEGS CROSS (2) KNEE-KNEE

Meaning: I am very relaxed.

Action: With the figure seated, the legs are crossed at the knees.

Background: This is the typical, social leg-cross posture. In Europe it is used by both men and women, but in America it is more confined to females. As a result, some of the more rugged American males find that the sight of European males sitting in this posture makes them uneasy. To their eyes, the posture is essentially effeminate.

Locality: Worldwide.

LEGS CROSS (3) ANKLE-KNEE

Meaning: I am assertively relaxed.

Action: With the figure seated, one ankle is brought up to rest on the knee of the other leg.

Background: This is a predominantly male form of leg-crossing. It is an aggressively masculine posture favoured especially by young males who wish to emphasize their gender. It originated as a 'cowboy' posture, related to their lifestyle and clothing. If used today by visitors to the Middle East it can cause offence. This is because it nearly always involves the display of the sole of a shoe, and this is considered a serious insult in that region. It would also be considered rather crude in eastern countries such as Thailand and Japan, where all forms of leg-crossing are rare.

Locality: Widespread in the Western world, but most common in the United States, especially in the Mid-West.

LEGS CURTSEY

Meaning: Formal subordination.

Action: One foot steps back while both legs are bent at the knee. The lowered position is held for only a moment.

Background: This is the 'intention movement' of kneeling. The figure starts to perform the kneel, but stops before the knees touch the ground. As an abbreviated kneel in medieval times, it became the common form of subordination for several centuries. In Shakespeare's day both men and women performed a bowing curtsey as a respectful greeting, but then the sexes separated, with the males bowing and only the females curtseying. Today the curtsey is restricted to highly formal occasions, usually involving royalty.

Locality: Europe, but rare.

LEGS TWINE

Meaning: I am slinkily relaxed.

Action: With the figure seated, one leg is twined tightly around the other.

Background: This is a female posture. Most males find it uncomfortable or even impossible to adopt this position of the legs. It therefore acts as a powerful, if unconscious gender signal. Because of the tight way in which the legs wrap around one another, it gives the impression of self-hugging and this adds a mild sexual quality to the posture.

Locality: Widespread.

LIP BITE

Meaning: I am angry.

Action: The gesturer bites his own lower lip with his teeth, shaking his head from side to side vigorously as he does so.

Locality: Widespread.

LIP TOUCH

Meaning: I want to talk to you.

Action: The tip of the forefinger touches the protruded lower lip several times.

Background: Like many simple gestures, this draws attention to part of the body by touching it. Because the mouth is used for talking, drinking, feeding and kissing, there can easily be misunderstandings here. In particular, this gesture may be confused with the Hand Purse that is used to indicate hunger. The difference is that here actual contact is made with the lower lip.

Locality: Greece.

LIPS KISS (1)

Meaning: Love.

Action: Mouth-to-mouth contact with the lips.

Background: Mouth-kissing, as a human sexual activity, is derived from the primeval action of passing food from the mouth of a mother to the mouth of her infant. Food-passing of this kind, which still occurs today in certain tribal societies, was part of the normal weaning process in earlier times. The lip contact involved became indelibly associated with loving care and, because of this, eventually became incorporated into the adult sexual sequence. It has sometimes been claimed that mouth-kissing is a local, western activity and that it is not worldwide, but this is an error. It has been found in every culture, right across the globe. The reason that it was mistakenly believed to be absent from certain societies is because it is not always permitted in public. In some Oriental cultures, for example, public kissing is considered vulgar, even today. There, it is confined strictly to the bedroom, as part of love-making. In the West, by contrast, prolonged kissing is now often seen on the streets of major cities. At its lowest intensity, the action is no more than the contact of closed lips, but at higher intensities it becomes open mouthed and may include exploration of the insides of the mouths with the tongues. In this respect, in particular, it mimics very clearly the food-passing of earlier days.

Locality: Worldwide.

LIPS KISS (2)

Meaning: She is sexy!

Action: The lips perform an air-kiss in the direction of an attractive female.

Background: Among English-speaking populations, the 'continental' Fingertips Kiss is often replaced by a long-distance air-kiss.

Locality: Most common in British Isles, but now widespread.

LIPS LICK

Meaning: Please kiss me.

Action: The tongue protrudes a short distance from the slightly opened lips and then moves slowly from one side of the mouth to the other.

Background: This is usually an invitation made by teenage boys towards girls.

Locality: North and South America.

LIPS POINT

Meaning: Indicating direction.

Action: The lips are protruded briefly in a particular direction. The action is emphasized by a slight turn of the head in the same direction.

Background: This method of pointing is used either because the hands are occupied or because the gesturer lives in a society where it is considered rude to point with the finger or hand.

Locality: The Philippines, parts of South and central America, certain African tribes, and among American Indians.

LIPS SEAL

Meaning: Don't say a word!

Action: The forefinger and thumb hold the lips tightly closed.

Background: This is a request for silence or secrecy and may sometimes be performed rather aggressively, with the unspoken threat that 'I will sew your lips together like this to keep you quiet.'

Locality: Southern Italy.

LIPS TOUCH

Meaning: Be quiet!

Action: The forefinger is brought up to the lips and held there for a moment.

Background: The finger symbolically blocks the source of speech.

Locality: Widespread.

LIPS ZIP

Meaning: Keep a secret.

Action: The erect thumb is moved smartly from one mouth-corner to the other, as if closing a zip fastener.

Background: The meaning of this gesture differs from the previous one. The pressing of the forefinger to the lips is usually a request for physical silence – 'Stop that noise'. The thumb action is more concerned with requesting that someone remains silent in the future, rather than the present. It may signal either 'I won't say anything' or 'Please don't say anything'.

Locality: The Americas.

LITTLE-FINGER ERECT (1)

Meaning: Bad.

Action: The hand is held up with only the little finger erect. The other fingers are held down by the thumb.

Background: The little finger is used here in contrast with the erect thumb which signifies 'good'.

Locality: Bali.

LITTLE-FINGER ERECT (2)

Meaning: Small penis.

Action: (As above)

Background: Here the little finger is a symbolic phallus. Being the most diminutive phallic symbol the hand has to offer, it acts as an obvious insult.

Locality: Widespread. Most common in the Mediterranean region.

LITTLE-FINGER ERECT (3)

Meaning: Thin.

Action: (As above)

Background: Here the small size of the little finger symbolizes thinness. It is usually employed as a 'thin' gesture in cases where someone is slender to the point of being ill, or where a girl is unattractively skinny.

Locality: Parts of Europe and South America.

LITTLE-FINGER ERECT (4)

Meaning: Female companion.

Action: (As above)

Background: Because it is slender, the little finger here symbolizes the female, contrasting with the thicker thumb, which is male. This version of the gesture is used to refer to a man's female companion, regardless of whether she is a girl friend, a mistress, or a wife.

Locality: Japan.

LITTLE-FINGER ERECT (5)

Meaning: I know your secret.

Action: The little finger is raised near the ear, with the head tilted, as if listening to it.

Background: This is the gesture summed up by the phrase 'A little bird told me'. The fact that it is also known as 'It's my little finger that told me' indicates that the erect finger is meant to symbolize a small bird perched near the ear, whispering secrets into it.

Locality: Europe, especially France.

LITTLE-FINGERS HOOK (1)

Meaning: He is crafty!

Action: The little fingers are hooked together.

Background: The gesture signifies that someone is 'well-connected'.

Locality: Italy, especially the Neapolitan region.

LITTLE-FINGERS HOOK (2)

Meaning: Friendship.

Action: The little fingers are hooked together.

Background: The hooking of the little fingers symbolizes the bond of friendship. This gesture is most often used by children. A variant employs the forefingers instead of the little fingers.

Locality: Widespread, but most commonly used by Arab children.

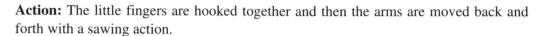

LITTLE-FINGERS SAW

Meaning: They are enemies.

Action: The little fingers are hooked together and then the arms are moved back and forth with a sawing action.

Background: This is a variant of the 'friendship' hooking of the little fingers, with the hands symbolizing two friends who are locked together in the to and fro of serious dispute.

Locality: Middle East.

LITTLE-FINGERS UNHOOK

Meaning: We are enemies.

Action: The hooked little fingers are torn apart.

Background: This is the gesture by which a friendship is ended. Mostly used by Arab children. A variant employs the forefingers instead of the little fingers.

Locality: Arab cultures.

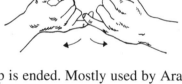

MIDDLE-FINGER BEND

Meaning: Insult.

Action: The forefinger of one hand bends the middle finger of the other hand backwards.

Background: This gesture is called 'Looking under the cat's tail'.

Locality: Russia.

MIDDLE-FINGER DOWN-PROD

Meaning: Sexual insult.

Action: The hand is extended, palm-down, with all the digits straight except the middle finger, which is bent downwards. In this position the hand is jerked down several times.

Background: This is a phallic gesture in which the middle finger symbolizes the thrusting penis.

Locality: Arab cultures.

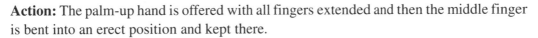

MIDDLE-FINGER ERECT

Meaning: Sexual insult.

Action: The palm-up hand is offered with all fingers extended and then the middle finger is bent into an erect position and kept there.

Background: As in the last gesture, the middle finger symbolizes the penis. In this case, however, there are no thrusting movements. The bending up of the finger mimes the moment of erection that occurs during sexual excitement.

Locality: Egypt.

MIDDLE-FINGER FLICKER

Meaning: You have a snake's tongue.

Action: The middle finger alone is straightened and then flickered up and down.

Background: The implication is that someone keeps chattering – flickering their tongue like a snake.

Locality: The Punjab.

MIDDLE-FINGER JERK (1)

Meaning: Sexual insult.

Action: The stiff middle finger is thrust upwards.

Background: With this well-known gesture, the middle finger symbolizes an erect penis. The other digits, curled on either side of it, represent the testicles. This is one of the oldest sexual insults known. It was popular in Ancient Rome and references to it occur in the works of classical authors. It was so notorious that the middle finger became known as the *digitus impudicus* – the indecent finger. The scandalous emperor Caligula is said to have extended his middle finger when offering his hand to be kissed, as a deliberate way of outraging his subjects.

Locality: Widespread; especially common in the United States, where it is known simply as 'the finger'.

MIDDLE-FINGER JERK (2)

Meaning: (As above)

Action: In this version of the gesture, instead of thrusting the finger upwards in the air, it is extended from the clenched fist at the very moment that the fist is slammed down into the palm of the other hand.

Background: This special variant of the gesture adds a slapping noise to the moment when the symbolic penis is thrust forward, as if the phallus is being forcibly rammed home. In other words, this version of 'the finger' gesture suggests rape, or violent copulation, rather than mere erection.

Locality: Lebanon and Syria.

MIDDLE-FINGER JERK (3)

Meaning: (As above)

Action: The middle finger is extended as the forearm is jerked upwards. The upward jerk is exaggerated by slamming the other hand down on to the arm-crook.

Background: This is a combination of the popular Forearm Jerk and the Middle-Finger Jerk, making it a doubly insulting gesture.

Locality: The Catholic regions of the Mediterranean – Spain, Portugal and Italy.

MIDDLE-FINGER PRESS

Meaning: Threat.

Action: The middle finger is pressed down by the thumb, with the other fingers held straight. In this position, the hand is then shaken in a downward chopping motion. The action is directed towards the threatened person.

Background: This is very similar to the Hand Chop threat, except that the finger involved is the middle one rather than the forefinger. The friendly American OK sign has been known to be mistaken for this.

Locality: Saudi Arabia.

MIDDLE-FINGER SUCK

Meaning: Sexual insult.

Action: The extended middle finger is pushed into the pursed lips, then withdrawn from the mouth and held erect.

Background: This is an obscene comment made by one man towards another, referring to the sexual activities of the women in his family. As before the middle finger acts as a symbolic penis.

Locality: Saudi Arabia.

MIDDLE-FINGERS PRESS

Meaning: I have slept with her.

Action: The palms are brought together with all digits bent except the middle fingers. These are extended forward and their tips are pressed together.

Background: The middle fingers symbolize two bodies pressed together in sexual contact. The gesture is performed towards a woman with whom the gesturer claims to have slept. This gesture carries a double message because the posture of the hands also forms the shape of female genitals.

Locality: Saudi Arabia.

MOUSTACHE TWIDDLE

Meaning: She is beautiful!

Action: The hands mime the action of twisting the ends of a waxed moustache.

Background: This is a relic gesture that has long outlived the style of moustache that inspired it. In the days when men wore moustaches with pointed, up-turned tips, made sharper by the application of wax, they would preen themselves when preparing for a flirtation. Today, even when completely clean-shaven, they still mime this action when they see a pretty girl walk past, as a way of saying to their companions, 'I must make myself ready to court her!'

Locality: Italy, especially Naples, and Greece.

MOUTH CLASP

Meaning: I should not have said that!

Action: The hand shoots up to cover the mouth.

Background: The action symbolically stops any more words being uttered.

Locality: Widespread. Especially common in Europe and the Americas.

MOUTH FAN

Meaning: My mouth is hot!

Action: The hand is fanned in front of the open mouth.

Background: The hand mimes the act of cooling the mouth. This fanning has no real impact on the condition of the mouth, but it signals to a companion that a particular dish or drink is very hot, either in the sense of temperature or spiciness.

Locality: Widespread.

MOUTH FIST

Meaning: I am thirsty.

Action: The thumb-side of the fist is placed against the lips.

Background: The gesture acts as a mime of drinking from a narrow-necked bottle held in the fist. It is a local variant of the more commonly seen tipped-glass Hand 'Drink' gesture.

Locality: Saudi Arabia.

MOUTH SALAAM

Meaning: Respect.

Action: The tips of the thumb and the first two fingers of the right hand are touched briefly to the lips, then waved slightly forwards and upwards into the air, while the head makes a bow.

Background: This is the most abbreviated form of the formal Arab greeting, the Salaam. In the full version, the hand goes first to the chest, then to the mouth and finally to the forehead, while the gesturer bows. The triple action symbolizes the message that 'I offer you my heart, my soul and my head.' In the less westernized Arab societies it replaces the more widespread greeting of the Hand Shake.

Locality: Arab cultures.

MOUTH SHRUG

Meaning: Disclaimer.

Action: The mouth corners are pulled down briefly, as far as possible.

Background: This is part of the 'shrug complex' that includes raised eyebrows, raised shoulders and spread palms. At close quarters it may be used by itself and then carries the same message as the full Shoulders Shrug. The message is 'I don't know', 'It's nothing to do with me', or 'I don't understand'.

Locality: Western world, with its strongest expression in France.

MOUTH SMILE

Meaning: Pleasure.

Action: The mouth corners are drawn back and at the same time are turned upwards.

Background: The smile is unique to the human species. It originates in infancy. The babies of monkeys and apes can cling on to their mother's fur, but our offspring need something else to help them stay close to the mother. Since they cannot cling on to her, they must make her want to stay very close to them. They do this by offering the appealing smile. In evolutionary terms, the smile is an expression of fear, as are all facial expressions that involve the pulling back of the lips. But this particular expression became subtly changed, from 'I am afraid' to 'I am not aggressive' to 'I am friendly'. In the process, it modified its shape slightly, which prevented any confusion between a friendly face and a frightened one. It did this by adding an upturning of the mouth corners as they are retracted. Today, if for some reason we revert to the original fearful smile, we find it hard to keep the mouth corners turned fully up. The result is the frozen, or nervous smile.

Locality: Worldwide.

MOUTH-AND-FOREHEAD SALAAM

Meaning: Respect.

Action: The tips of the thumb and the first two fingers of the right hand are touched briefly to the lips and then to the centre of the forehead, while the head makes a slight bow. The action ends with an upward and forward flourish of the hand.

Background: This is the moderate version of the full Arab greeting, the Salaam. In the full version, the chest is touched first, then the mouth, then the forehead. In this shortened version, the initial chest element is omitted. It is often accompanied by the pronouncement: 'Salaam alaykum' – 'Peace be with you'.

Locality: Arab cultures.

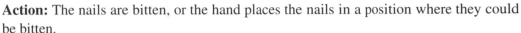

NAIL BITE

Meaning: I am anxious.

Action: The nails are bitten, or the hand places the nails in a position where they could be bitten.

Background: Placing fingers in the mouth is a sign that someone is stressed and needs comfort. This is an unconscious gesture that appears automatically when someone is under pressure. In origin, this gesture is a reversion to infancy, when oral pleasures were paramount. Many children suck their thumbs as a substitute for feeding at the breast, but this action is too 'juvenile' for any adult who happens to have the same need for oral comfort. Something less obvious is needed and 'fingers-in-the-mouth' takes its place. Once they are there, the tension of the stressed situation may lead to the actual biting of the nails.

Locality: Widespread.

NECK CLAMP

Meaning: I am angry.

Action: The hand swings up abruptly to clamp itself hard on to the nape of the neck.

Background: This unconscious action is a telltale sign of suddenly aroused, but otherwise unexpressed anger. When a companion makes an infuriating remark, it creates a powerful urge to hit him over the head. The overarm blow is the primeval attack movement of our species and it is automatically triggered off by a hostile comment. However, social inhibitions prevent us from carrying the action through in a primitive manner. We inhibit it, but not completely. The arm rises rapidly, as if about to strike the downward blow, but then we manage to check it. At that moment, the hand is close to the back of the head and we mask our action by clamping the nape of the neck or scratching the hair there. All of this is carried out in a split second without our being aware of what we are doing. Our irritating companion, preoccupied with his comments, may also ignore this small but vital clue that he has angered us.

Locality: Worldwide.

NECK CLASP

Meaning: What a disaster!

Action: The hand clasps the neck behind the ear.

Background: This is an act of self-comfort, the gesturer clasping himself behind his ear, as though giving himself a consoling hug.

Locality: Jewish communities.

NECK FLICK

Meaning: Join me for a drink.

Action: The forefinger is flicked against the neck.

Background: This is a familiar gesture, only used between old friends. It is considered rude if employed by a stranger.

Locality: Poland.

NECK KISS

Meaning: I love you.

Action: The companion's neck is gently kissed.

Background: Of all the kisses available, in a wide variety of social contexts, the Neck Kiss is essentially the lovers' kiss. It is even more intimate than the mouth-to-mouth kiss, partly because the neck-skin is so sensitive and partly because it suggests the start of a descent from public facial kissing to private body kissing.

Locality: European in origin but now widespread.

NECK RUB

Meaning: Sexual interest.

Action: The hand rubs the back of the neck.

Background: The action is performed by a man who sees an attractive woman and wishes to indicate that he would like to meet her.

Locality: Lebanon.

NECK SCRATCH

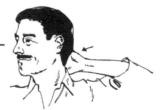

Meaning: Uncertainty.

Action: The side of the neck, just below the ear, is scratched several times with the forefinger.

Background: This is an unconscious gesture that is made by someone who is not sure of himself or who doubts what is being said, and does not like to say so.

Locality: Widespread.

NECK TAP

Meaning: Homosexual.

Action: The back of the neck is tapped lightly with the hand.

Locality: Lebanon.

NOSE BITE

Meaning: Sexual excitement.

Action: The nose of the companion is gently bitten during sexual foreplay.

Background: This is an erotic action employed during the later stages of pre-copulatory behaviour. It follows an initial period of arousal during which there is a great deal of hugging and nuzzling. Then, when both partners have become aroused, they begin nipping one another with their teeth, concentrating in particular on the facial region, especially the nose.

Locality: Trobriand Islands.

NOSE BRUSH

Meaning: We do not get on.

Action: The forefinger brushes the side of the nose.

Background: The nose is brushed to suggest that the gesturer has bad relations with someone.

Locality: Greece.

NOSE CIRCLE (1)

Meaning: Homosexual.

Action: One hand is brought up to the nose, where it encircles the nose-tip. This 'Hand Ring' is placed on to the nose and is then rotated, clockwise and anti-clockwise, as if the nose is trying to insert itself deeper into the 'tunnel' of the hand.

Background: This is a symbolic gesture that is meant to represent the act of anal penetration, with the nose as penis and the hand as anus. It is a North American gesture signifying that someone is homosexual and is usually employed as an obscene insult.

Locality: North America.

NOSE CIRCLE (2)

Meaning: You are a toady.

Action: (As above)

Background: In this second meaning the symbolism is slightly different. The hand still represents the anus, but the nose now stands for itself instead of for the penis. This gesture, known as 'Brown-nosing', implies that someone is a servile flatterer, so fawningly anxious to impress his superior that he engages in 'arse-licking', this action being caricatured as the pressing of the nose into the anus of the dominant individual.

Locality: North America.

NOSE CLASP-RUB

Meaning: Clever.

Action: The nose is lightly held between the tips of the thumb and forefinger of one hand. The ridge of the nose is then rubbed up and down several times.

Background: In origin, this gesture is a mimic action, imitating the way in which a scholarly person rubs his nose after removing his spectacles, following a long bout of intense study.

Locality: Italy.

NOSE DRILL

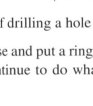

Meaning: I defy you!

Action: The forefinger is twisted into the side of the nose, as if drilling a hole in it.

Background: This gesture says 'You can drill a hole in my nose and put a ring in it, like a bull, but you will still not be able to control me. I will continue to do what I want, despite you.'

Locality: Greece.

NOSE FAN

Meaning: It stinks!

Action: The horizontal index finger is moved up and down beneath the nostrils, as if trying to fan a bad smell away from the nose.

172

Background: This stylized form of air-fanning is used to signal that something stinks, either literally or metaphorically.

Locality: South America.

NOSE FLARE

Meaning: Anger.

Action: The nostrils are flared as a result of contraction of the muscles on either side of the nose. The flaring usually accompanies a sharp intake of breath.

Background: This expression is observed at moments of sudden outrage or exasperation. It appears to be an unconscious gesture common to all human societies.

Locality: Worldwide.

NOSE FLICK

Meaning: Homosexual.

Action: The extended forefinger of the right hand flicks the tip of the nose.

Background: The gesture signifies that the man towards whom the action is directed is a homosexual. In origin, the Nose Flick is probably similar to the Ear Flick, which carries the same message. In the case of the Ear Flick, the message is 'You should be wearing earrings'. The Nose Flick has been observed in countries where it was traditional for women to wear nose-ornaments similar to earrings.

Locality: Syria and the Lebanon.

NOSE HOLD

Meaning: Bad!

Action: The nostrils are squeezed tightly between the thumb and forefinger.

Background: A deliberate symbolic gesture, signifying that something is bad or a failure, based on the idea that something 'stinks' and the nostrils must be protected from the stench. A British elaboration of this common gesture involves pulling an imaginary lavatory chain with the left hand while the right hand holds the nose.

Locality: Widespread.

NOSE HOOK

Meaning: Defiance.

Action: The forefinger of the right hand is hooked over the nose, while the rest of the hand is clenched.

Background: This is a gesture of disobedience, the message being 'I will do it in spite of you'.

Locality: Saudi Arabia.

NOSE KISS

Meaning: I am sorry.

Action: The lips kiss the tip of the nose of a companion.

Background: This action is observed after a dispute, when one person wishes to apologize to the other.

Locality: Saudi Arabia.

NOSE LIFT

Meaning: It is easy!

Action: The first two fingers lift the nose by pushing the nostrils upwards.

Background: This gesture originates from the idea that something 'is so easy I could do it with my fingers up my nose'.

Locality: France.

NOSE PICK

Meaning: Insult.

Action: A finger is inserted into one nostril and used to pick clean the interior.

Background: Because there is a mild social taboo about employing this action in public, it is used as a deliberate insult in some regions. This is common in some Arab cultures, where it is performed in a stylized way. There, the forefinger and thumb of the right hand are inserted simultaneously into the nostrils. They are then flicked forward towards the insulted person, with the silent message 'go to hell!'

Locality: Libya and Syria.

NOSE PINCH

Meaning: You make me sick!

Action: The nose is pinched shut by the fingers and the tongue protrudes from the open mouth. The gesture is sometimes accompanied by a vomiting sound.

Background: By pretending to vomit, the gesturer makes a powerful comment on the behaviour, appearance, or opinion of a companion.

Locality: Common in the Western world, especially among children.

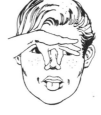

NOSE POINT

Meaning: Myself.

Action: The forefinger points directly at the tip of the nose.

Background: In the West, when a speaker refers to himself, he usually points at his chest. In the East this gesture may be directed instead at the nose.

Locality: Japan.

NOSE PULL

Meaning: I will punish you.

Action: The nose is gripped between the thumb and forefinger and pulled forward, as if someone else is tugging at it.

Background: A mimic gesture, employed as a threat of physical punishment.

Locality: South America.

NOSE PUSH (1)

Meaning: Threat of attack.

Action: The tip of the nose is pressed down and squashed flat with the extended right forefinger.

Background: This Arab gesture makes it clear that, unless the threat is heeded, a blow will follow, and the other person's nose will be broken and permanently flattened.

Locality: Saudi Arabia.

NOSE PUSH (2)

Meaning: Racist insult.

Action: (As above)

Background: In a different context, an identical Nose Push gesture is used as a racist insult by Arab against Negro, the squashing of the nose emphasizing the marked difference between the long, high-ridged Arab nose and the flatter, broader Negro nose.

Locality: Saudi Arabia.

NOSE ROCK

Meaning: Friendship.

Action: The back of the hand is pressed to the nose as the head is rocked up and down.

Background: The gesture mimes the action of a Nose Rub (1) greeting, with the hand representing the head of the friend.

Locality: Saudi Arabia.

NOSE RUB (1)

Meaning: Friendly welcome.

Action: The tip of the nose is brought into contact with the body of another person as a stylized form of greeting. Usually this greeting is performed nose-tip to nose-tip, but there are variations. Sometimes the nose is pressed into the cheek of the other person, or on to their head. The gesture signifies affection or, in a more formal setting, respectful friendliness. In its more intimate role, it becomes an action of mutual nose-rubbing. Because of this, it has become widely known as the 'nose-rubbing' greeting, despite the fact that in its more formal role it is usually abbreviated to no more than a fleeting nose-press or nose-tip-touch.

Background: As a modern greeting, nose contact is rare, compared with the Cheek Kiss, the Embrace and the Hand Shake, but it still survives in certain cultures. In origin, it harks back to the time when the nose was used to sniff the body of a returning companion. Although we are not always aware of it today, we are capable of identifying our loved ones and our close companions by their individual body fragrance. Mothers and babies are capable of identifying one another in this way within a few days of the arrival of the newborn. Greeting someone by sniffing them was done, not only to re-check their identity, but also to explore any changes in fragrance that had occurred during the period of separation. It has recently been discovered that our sensitivity to personal fragrance is centred in a small cavity inside the nose that acts as a specialized scent-detector. We are not conscious of the odours it detects, but we nevertheless register them and remember them.

Locality: Observed among the Maoris in New Zealand, the Lapps in Finland and the Bedouin of North Africa and Arabia. It is also performed by some Malays, Polynesians, Melanesians and Eskimos. It has also been claimed that Nose Rubbing was used in ancient Egypt, because their word 'sn' meant both 'kiss' and 'smell', but the evidence is weak.

NOSE RUB (2)

Meaning: Sexual invitation to a woman.

Action: The side of the forefinger is rubbed across the bridge of the nose.

Locality: Jordan.

NOSE SCREW (I)

Meaning: Drunk.

Action: The thumb and forefinger make a ring which encircles the nose. The hand is then screwed round through an arc.

Background: This is a Gallic gesture indicating to a companion that someone else is hopelessly drunk. It should not be confused with the Nose Circle.

Locality: France.

NOSE SCREW (2)

Meaning: Never mind!

Action: (As above)

Background: For most people, wiping the nose is a simple cleaning or comfort action, but in some regions it is also used as a specific signal. In such cases it sends the message: 'It doesn't matter' or 'It's not important'. When it does this it is performed in a stylized way, with the hand making a screwing movement around the nose, followed by a wiping action and a noisy exhalation. The gesture implies that a problem, like mucus from the nose, is best discarded and forgotten.

Locality: East Africa.

NOSE SNIFF

Meaning: Cocaine.

Action: The horizontal forefinger is brought up to touch the nostrils and then the back of the finger is swept sideways, keeping contact with the underside of the nose. As this movement is made it is accompanied by a loud sniffing noise.

Background: This is a mimic gesture that imitates the action of snorting cocaine. It signals either the desire for, or the possession of, cocaine.

Locality: Peru.

NOSE SNUB

Meaning: No thanks, it is beneath me.

Action: The tip of the forefinger presses the nose upwards.

Background: This action is employed as a contemptuous refusal. In origin, it is a theatrically mimed 'nose in the air', conveying snobbish superiority.

Locality: Central and Eastern Europe.

NOSE STROKE (1)

Meaning: I am broke.

Action: The extended forefinger and middle finger are stroked down the length of the nose, from the bridge to the tip.

Background: This gesture signifies that the performer has no money. It can be employed either as a statement of fact or as a request for help.

Locality: Portugal and Spain.

NOSE STROKE (2)

Meaning: He is mean.

Action: The extended forefinger is stroked down the length of the nose, from the bridge to the tip.

Background: This gesture is used when someone is thought to be stingy or cheap. It appears to be related to the Nose Stroke (1) gesture and may date back to the time when there was a Spanish presence in the Netherlands in the fifteenth and sixteenth centuries.

Locality: Holland.

NOSE TAP (1)

Meaning: Complicity.

Action: The side of the nose is tapped several times with a vertically held forefinger.

Background: This widespread signal is nearly always an indication that someone is 'sniffing something out'. Its message is one of 'alertness', but the exact form that this takes varies from place to place. One version signals that 'you and I share a secret which we must guard because others will try to sniff it out.'

Locality: English-speaking and Italian-speaking regions.

NOSE TAP (2)

Meaning: Be alert!

Action: (As above)

Background: An alternative meaning is that someone is nosing about and we must be alert to their presence. This friendly warning differs from the Complicity form only in that there is no shared secret involved.

Locality: Italy.

NOSE TAP (3)

Meaning: You are nosey!

Action: (As above)

Background: This is a direct accusation towards a person believed to be 'sticking his nose' into your business. Its message is 'keep your nose out of my affairs'.

Locality: Common in the British Isles, especially in Wales.

NOSE TAP (4)

Meaning: I am alert!

Action: (As above)

Background: The message is 'I know what is going on – I can sniff it out.'

Locality: Found in many regions but is most commonly used in the Flemish-speaking region of Belgium.

NOSE TAP (5)

Meaning: He is clever!

Action: (As above)

Background: The nose-tapper is signalling that someone else is good at sniffing out the truth.

Locality: Largely southern Italy.

NOSE TAP (6)

Meaning: Threat.

Action: (As above)

Background: A minor, but widespread use of the Nose Tap is to signal a threat: 'I have sniffed out what you are up to and if you do not stop I will attack you.'

Locality: Widespread.

All these six meanings of the Nose Tap are closely related, but their existence reveals the way in which a simple gesture can gradually start to alter its significance in different regions, as local traditions become established.

NOSE THUMB (I) ONE-HANDED

Meaning: Playful insult.

Action: The tip of the thumb is placed on the end of the nose, with the hand held vertically and the fingers spread in a fan. The fingers may be held still or waggled back and forth.

Background: This is an ancient gesture – at least five hundred years old – known throughout all of Europe and the Americas and in many other regions. It has one basic message that is understood everywhere: mockery. Its origin is obscure. It has been interpreted as a deformed salute, a grotesque nose, a phallic nose, a threat of snot-flicking, and the display of an aggressive cock's comb, but its roots go so far back that nobody can be certain. Because it has such a long history it has acquired more names than any other gesture. These include the following: To thumb the nose, To make a nose, To cock a snook, To pull a snook, To cut a snooks, To make a long nose, Taking a sight, Taking a double sight, The Shanghai gesture, Queen Anne's fan, The Japanese fan, The Spanish fan, To pull bacon, Coffee-milling, To take a grinder, The five-finger salute; in France: Pied de nez, Un pan de nez, Le nez long; in Italy: Marameo, Maramau, Palmo di naso, Tanto di naso, Naso lungo; in Germany: Die lange Nase, Atsch! Atsch!

Locality: Widespread.

NOSE THUMB (2) TWO-HANDED

Meaning: Playful insult.

Action: As above, but with the other hand added to make a double 'fan'.

Background: This two-handed version has the same history as the single-handed. It is used for greater emphasis of the message.

Locality: Widespread.

NOSE TIP-TOUCH

Meaning: I promise.

Action: The tip of the extended right forefinger is placed on the tip of the nose. As this is done, the performer says 'On my nose!'

Background: This is an Arab gesture which signifies a solemn commitment to do something. In origin, it is related to the ancient custom of touching the genitals when swearing an oath. In this instance, the nose is acting as a symbolic substitute for the penis.

Locality: Libya, Saudi Arabia and Syria.

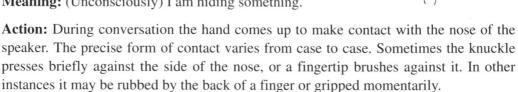

NOSE TOUCH

Meaning: (Unconsciously) I am hiding something.

Action: During conversation the hand comes up to make contact with the nose of the speaker. The precise form of contact varies from case to case. Sometimes the knuckle presses briefly against the side of the nose, or a fingertip brushes against it. In other instances it may be rubbed by the back of a finger or gripped momentarily.

Background: Touching the nose unknowingly in this way during a verbal encounter often signals deceit. The person performing the action is unaware of it, which makes it a valuable clue as to their true feelings. Why unconscious nose-touching should be closely linked with telling lies is not clear, but it may be that, at the moment of deceit the hand makes an involuntary move to cover the mouth – to hide the lie, as it were – and then moves on to the nose. The final shift from mouth to nose may be due to an unconscious sensation that mouth-covering is too obvious – something that every child does when telling untruths. Touching the nose, as if it is itching, may therefore be a disguised mouth-cover – a cover-up of the cover-up. However, some individuals report that they have felt a genuine sensation of nose tingling or itching at the very moment they have been forced to tell a lie, so that the action may be caused by some kind of small physiological change in the nasal tissue, as a result of the fleeting stress of the deceit. It should be noted that not all involuntary nose-touching indicates actual lying. It may, in a few instances, reveal that a person was considering lying, but then finally decided to tell the truth. What all cases of involuntary nose-touching do have in common is that, at the moment the action takes place, the performer is reacting emotionally to the situation being faced, even though outwardly they appear calm. The inner thoughts are seething, while a decision is made to lie or, with difficulty, to tell the truth. It is that inner turmoil, following a difficult question from a companion, which the Nose Touch reveals.

Locality: Worldwide.

NOSE TRIPLE-TOUCH

Meaning: Friendly welcome.

Action: The nose-tips of two men are brought together and touched three times in quick succession as a form of greeting.

Background: This is a stylized version of the ordinary Nose Rub (1) greeting and is employed between men of the nomadic Bedouin tribes. Their triple-touch is followed by lip-smacking.

Locality: Saudi Arabia.

NOSE TWIST

Meaning: Disapproval.

Action: The nose is twisted briefly to one side.

Background: This small movement signifies that the gesturer has just heard or seen something that has aroused disbelief or dislike. In origin, it is a symbolic turning-away of the nose from an unpleasant odour, but is a less extreme comment than the full Nose Wrinkle.

Locality: Widespread.

NOSE UP

Meaning: Superiority.

Action: The position of the nose is raised by tilting the head backwards.

Background: This action signifies dominance, defiance or contempt. It is the gesture of someone who feels a momentary need to reinforce their high status by a token display of body-heightening. The Nose Up posture reveals that for some reason their superiority is not being fully recognized and therefore requires a slight reinforcement. The upward movement of the nose produces the opposite effect of the subordinate or shy lowering of the head. Usually seen as an unconscious gesture during social interactions, the Nose Up action has given rise to three popular expressions: having one's 'nose-in-the-air', 'turning up one's nose' at something, and 'looking down your nose' at someone. It may also be the origin of the term 'stuck-up', meaning snobbish. Because these expressions exist, the action may sometimes be performed deliberately. When this occurs it is nearly always employed theatrically as a joking, mock-supercilious gesture. (It has also been described as a Chin Lift gesture.)

Locality: Worldwide.

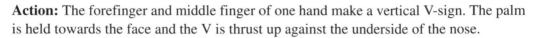

NOSE V

Meaning: Obscene insult.

Action: The forefinger and middle finger of one hand make a vertical V-sign. The palm is held towards the face and the V is thrust up against the underside of the nose.

Background: This symbolic gesture is a sexual insult, the nose representing the penis and the finger-V the vagina. It should not be confused with the 'cigarette request gesture' which mimes the act of bringing a cigarette up to the mouth.

Locality: Saudi Arabia and Mexico.

NOSE WIGGLE

Meaning: What is happening?

Action: The nose is wiggled from side to side.

Background: In some countries this is used as a way of asking a question. In origin, it derives from the idea that 'I can smell something strange, but I cannot tell what it is.'

Locality: Common in Puerto Rico.

NOSE WIPE

Meaning: Too late!

Action: The forefinger, pointing sideways, is slid under the nose.

Background: This gesture is known as 'Under the nose' ('Sous le nez') or simply 'Pfuit'. It is a stylized form of nose-wiping used to signal that the gesturer is too late for something and has just missed it.

Locality: France.

NOSE WOBBLE

Meaning: I do not trust you.

Action: The first two fingers, placed one on either side of the nose, wobble it from side to side.

Background: The gesture implies that something stinks and the gesturer is trying to get the stench out of his nostrils.

Locality: Southern Italy.

NOSE WRINKLE

Meaning: Disgust.

Action: The muscles on either side of the nose are tightened to shorten it, creating wrinkle lines between the eyes.

Background: Based on the nose's reaction to smelling something unpleasant, this gesture signifies a wide range of distaste, from mild disapproval to intense disgust.

Locality: Worldwide.

PALM CUP

Meaning: Disclaimer.

Action: The hand is raised to shoulder height with the cupped palm facing forward. At the same time the shoulders perform a slight shrugging movement.

Background: This is a special version of the shrug in which the hand is raised instead of being held forward.

Locality: France.

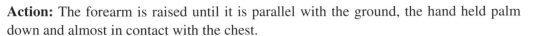

PALM DOWN

Meaning: It's fine.

Action: The forearm is raised until it is parallel with the ground, the hand held palm down and almost in contact with the chest.

Background: This gesture means that something is good, delicate or fine. It carries the message 'Es muy delicado'.

Locality: South America.

PALM FLIP

Meaning: Swearing an oath.

Action: The palm of the right hand is flipped up and over the right shoulder. At the same time the head is tilted back a little and the eyes are raised up.

Locality: Libya, Lebanon and Syria.

PALM GRIND (1)

Meaning: Obscenity.

Action: The back of the right hand is rubbed into the palm of the left hand with a rhythmic, grinding motion.

Background: The gesture symbolizes the grinding movements of copulation, with each hand representing one of the bodies involved.

Locality: Lebanon.

PALM GRIND (2)

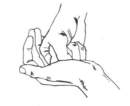

Meaning: You are squashed!

Action: (As above)

Locality: Spain.

PALM HIGH-SLAP

Meaning: Congratulations.

Action: The palms of the raised right hands are slapped together, hard.

Background: At a moment of triumph, when the ordinary Hand Shake seems a little tame, various more flamboyant alternatives have recently been introduced, especially in sport. These are more showy and more violent, as befits the context. The clasping of the hand in the Hand Shake was first replaced by the 'give me five' Palm Slap, in which one person holds out a hand, palm-up, and the companion slaps down on it hard, with the reverse then taking place. This was then taken a step further with the 'high five' in which one person raises an arm and holds the palm high in the air, again demanding 'give me five'. The other person must then reach up with a high hand-slap, after which he offers his own hand for the same treatment. In the most exaggerated gesture of all, the two companions both leap high in the air with simultaneously raised right hands, slapping them together at the maximum height possible, while their feet are off the ground. These gestures had their beginnings in American Football, but have since spread to other sports and even to ordinary social occasions.

Locality: United States, but spreading rapidly.

PALM KISS

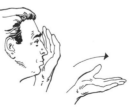

Meaning: I love you.

Action: The palm is kissed and then extended towards the companion.

Background: This is a variant of the Fingertips Kiss. It has a slightly more intimate flavour, resulting from the pressing of the lips to the smooth flesh of the palm.

Locality: Widespread.

188

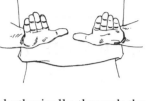

PALM LOWER

Meaning: Less, please.

Action: The palm, facing down, is lowered several times rhythmically through the air. Or both palms may be lowered together in this way.

Background: This common gesture mimes the act of gently pressing something lower and is used to request less of something. According to context, this can mean: violent action reduced to calm; loud noises reduced to silence; or high speed reduced to low speed.

Locality: Widespread.

PALM PLUCK

Meaning: Lazy!

Action: The thumb and forefinger of one hand pluck an imaginary hair from the centre of the palm of the other hand.

Background: The gesture is based on the idea that 'he is so lazy that a hair could grow on his palm.'

Locality: France.

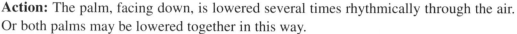

PALM POINT

Meaning: Disbelief.

Action: The forefinger points at the centre of the palm of the other hand.

Background: The message of the gesture is that 'grass will grow here on the palm of my hand before what you are telling me comes true.'

Locality: Israel and other Jewish communities.

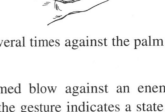

PALM PUNCH (1)

Meaning: Anger.

Action: The fist of one hand is punched rhythmically several times against the palm of the other.

Background: This has a common meaning of a mimed blow against an enemy, redirected on to the palm of the gesturer. In such cases the gesture indicates a state of barely controlled rage.

Locality: Widespread.

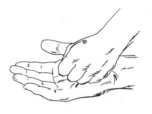

PALM PUNCH (2)

Meaning: Invitation to sex.

Action: (As above, but with a slightly smoother, faster beat.)

Background: The Palm Punch also has an additional, special meaning in certain cultures, where it is used as a sexual signal. There, it indicates a desire on the part of the male gesturer to sleep with the woman to whom he directs the action. In these instances the rhythmic blows mime the action of pelvic thrusting during copulation.

Locality: Middle East.

PALM PUNCH (3)

Meaning: Agreed!

Action: The palm is punched hard, once, by the fist of the other hand. This version of the gesture differs in that it is not the knuckles but the bent fingers that are struck against the palm.

Background: This is a gesture that seals a negotiation in the market place.

Locality: West Africa.

PALM SCRAPE

Meaning: Money.

Action: The fingertips of one hand are scraped lightly over the palm of the other hand. The action is repeated several times.

Background: The action mimics scooping money into the hand.

Locality: Widespread, but most common in South America.

PALM SCREW

Meaning: Sexual insult.

Action: The stiff right forefinger is screwed into the palm of the right hand.

Background: The forefinger symbolizes the active penis.

Locality: Middle East.

PALM SHOW

Meaning: I swear!

Action: The right hand is raised to the level of the shoulder and held there with the palm facing forward.

Background: This is done by both Moslems and Christians when swearing an oath.

Locality: Widespread.

PALM SLAP

Meaning: Celebration.

Action: Two companions slap their right palms together. This is initiated by one person holding out the right hand, palm up, inviting it to be slapped.

Background: Although this may be used as a greeting in place of the more usual Hand Shake, it is more commonly observed at a moment of celebration, especially in a sporting context, or when a 'point' has been scored in a social context. In origin, it is an exaggeration of the initial element of the Hand Shake, when the palms come together. But instead of clasping the hands and shaking them up and down, they are forcibly struck against one another. The gesture is often preceded by the request 'Give me five!'

Locality: Originally a male American gesture, it has recently spread to other parts of the world, via cinema and television.

PALM THRUST

Meaning: Go to hell!

Action: The palm is thrust towards the companion, as if pushing something into his face.

Background: This is an ancient Byzantine gesture dating from the time when criminals were chained up and put on display in the streets. It was the custom for local tormentors to pick up a handful of filth and push it into the face of these helpless captives. This action has survived into modern times as a symbolic gesture, in which the handful of filth is imaginary and the victim is someone who has simply caused annoyance. A popular insult between drivers in traffic jams, it is known as the Moutza gesture. With many people who use it today, its ancient origin has been completely forgotten, but it retains its powerful message none the less. Like many ancient gestures, it has acquired a modern 'explanation'. As in other cases, this invented explanation is sexual in nature. In this particular case, it states that the five digits displayed by the thrust hand represent five different sexual acts the gesturer would like to perform with the victim's sister. This interpretation helps to keep the gesture alive in present day Greece. For foreign visitors who are unfamiliar with the Moutza, there is a constant risk that a simple hand signal, requesting that someone should move back, could be misunderstood as the viciously insulting Moutza.

Locality: Greece.

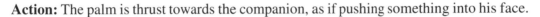

PALM THUMB

Meaning: You must pay!

Action: The thumb of one hand is stroked down the palm of the other, from wrist to fingertips.

Background: The message is 'pay up!', the thumb mimicking the action of money being placed on the hand.

Locality: Holland.

PALM TICKLE

Meaning: Sexual proposition.

Action: When shaking hands a man tickles his companion's palm with his forefinger.

Background: An uninhibited sexual gesture largely employed by teenagers.

Locality: Widespread.

PALM UP (1)

Meaning: Please give me.

Action: One hand is stretched forward and held in the palm-up position. The palm is slightly cupped. Usually aimed directly at another person.

Background: This is the typical begging posture of the human species and can also be seen in our closest relatives, the Great Apes. The palm-up position of the hand invites a companion to place something in it, nearly always food or money. With professional street-beggars, the action may become undirected, the outstretched hand remaining in a fixed position for long periods of time, without any orientation towards approaching figures.

Locality: Worldwide.

PALM UP (2)

Meaning: Pay up!

Action: Similar to the begging gesture, but with the palm flatter and the thumb held stiffly out to the side.

Background: This is the dominant version of the begging hand, with the request for help replaced by a stern demand.

Locality: Worldwide.

PALMS BACK

Meaning: I embrace you.

Action: A speaker holds his hands forward, but with the palms facing his own body.

Background: A speaker who wishes to embrace an audience with his ideas sometimes unconsciously adopts an embracing posture with his arms and hands.

Locality: Worldwide.

PALMS BRUSH

Meaning: I have finished with it.

Action: The hands move up and down alternately, with the palms brushing against one another as they pass.

Background: The gesture mimes the act of brushing dirt from the hands at the conclusion of a task. Its message is that the performer now 'washes his hands' of something or someone.

Locality: Widespread.

PALMS CONTACT (I)

Meaning: Prayer.

Action: The palms are pressed together, fingers pointing upwards, in front of the body.

Background: This posture of prayer originated as a mime of the bound hands of a captive. The praying person is saying, in effect, I offer myself to God as his slave. Today, most people are unaware of this ancient origin, but the posture has survived as the traditional gesture of the pious and the faithful. Almost everywhere it has replaced the even more ancient prayer posture of raised arms, in which the supplicant reaches up towards the heavens.

Locality: Widespread, especially in the Western world.

PALMS CONTACT (2)

Meaning: Greeting.

Action: As above, but usually accompanied by a slight bow of the head.

Background: In the East, this form of greeting takes the place of the more widespread Western Hand Shake.

Locality: An Asiatic greeting, known in India as the Namaste and in Thailand as the Wai.

PALMS CONTACT (3)

Meaning: Thank you.

Action: (As above)

Background: In cultures where this gesture is employed as a greeting it is also employed as a way of expressing gratitude.

Locality: Asia.

PALMS CONTACT (4)

Meaning: Apology.

Action: (As above)

Background: In both East and West this gesture is used to ask forgiveness.

Locality: Widespread.

PALMS DOWN

Meaning: Calm down.

Action: A speaker holds his arms forward with the palms facing downwards. In this posture he may make small downbeats with his hands.

Background: A speaker who wishes to 'hold down' an idea or reduce the mood of his audience may adopt this hand posture, miming the act of physically pressing them down. If calming his audience becomes more urgent, he may increase the downbeat element. He will also strengthen the downbeat if he wishes them to lower themselves physically – the 'please be seated' gesture.

Locality: Worldwide.

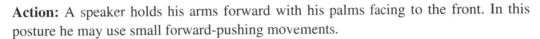

PALMS FRONT

Meaning: I hold you back.

Action: A speaker holds his arms forward with his palms facing to the front. In this posture he may use small forward-pushing movements.

Background: A speaker who is disagreeing with his audience, rejecting their ideas, or trying to repel their arguments, may adopt this posture, miming the action of pushing them away from him. As an accompaniment to a speech, he may adopt this posture unconsciously. Alternatively, he may use it deliberately, with more obvious pushing actions, if he wishes people to move backwards physically – the 'go back!' gesture.

Locality: Worldwide, except for Greece, where this action is too similar to the grossly insulting Palms Thrust or double Moutza gesture.

PALMS RUB (I)

Meaning: Regret.

Action: The slightly curled palms are rubbed hard together.

Background: This gesture is a survivor from ancient times, when it was commonplace to 'wring one's hands with grief'.

Locality: Saudi Arabia.

PALMS RUB (2)

Meaning: They are lesbians.

Action: The flattened palms are rubbed together.

Background: In this version of the gesture the rubbing movements are made directly forward and back, as if two bodies are sliding up against one another. The basis of the symbolism is that sexual contact movements are being made between two people, but without any phallic element.

Locality: South America.

PALMS THRUST

Meaning: Go to hell twice!

Action: The palms are thrust forward towards the companion, as if pushing something into his face.

Background: This is the Double Moutza, employed as a gross insult. Its origin is the same as the Palm Thrust, of which it is merely an amplified version.

Locality: Greece.

PALMS UP (I)

Meaning: I implore you.

Action: The hands reach towards the companion with the palms facing upward. They are then held in this position while the gesturer continues to speak.

Background: This is a common device of public speakers who wish to beg their audience to agree with them. As they make their plea they unconsciously adopt the human begging posture with both their hands.

Locality: Worldwide.

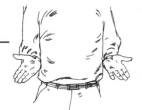

PALMS UP (2)

Meaning: I swear!

Action: Similar to the above action, but with the important difference that the palm-up hands do not reach forward but are instead placed against the gesturer's sides. At the same time the head is tilted backwards.

Background: This is essentially a religious gesture in which the performer gazes up to heaven and implores the deity to witness the swearing of an oath.

Locality: Middle East, including Jordan, Lebanon, Libya, Syria and Saudi Arabia.

PALMS UP (3)

Meaning: Prayer.

Action: Similar to (2) above, but with hands more forward and the head or eyes lowered.

Background: This is a ceremonial posture of prayer in which the devout call upon the deity for help.

Locality: Certain religious sects.

PALMS 'WASH'

Meaning: Anticipation.

Action: The palms are rubbed together as if washing them, despite the fact that they are dry.

Background: Many people unconsciously start to 'wash' their dry hands when they are anticipating something pleasant. The timing of this action has nothing to do with real washing or with the presence of dirt on the hands. It is often seen when a diner walks to his table in a restaurant, or when someone arrives at an exciting event and impatiently awaits the start of proceedings.

Locality: Widespread.

PALMS WIPE

Meaning: Finished!

Action: The palms are wiped over one another, alternately, several times.

Background: The action symbolically removes all traces of something from the palms of the hand, with the message 'I wash my hands of that'. It is used during conversations to indicate that something is over and done with, of no further interest, finished with or completed.

Locality: Widespread.

PUPILS DILATE

Meaning: I like what I see.

Action: The pupils of the eyes enlarge excessively.

Background: The pupils respond to the amount of light falling upon them, rather in the way that we adjust the lens aperture on a camera. In bright light they become pinpricks. In dim light they expand to increase the illumination of the retina. But sometimes they disobey this rule and enlarge more than they should do, for the amount of light falling upon them. This happens when we see something we like so much that we become emotionally aroused. It occurs unconsciously and automatically. Because we are incapable of controlling this response, it is a valuable way of measuring our reaction to one another and to various other images. Our pupils dilate strongly when we are falling in love and find ourselves gazing deeply at our companion. They also dilate when we see something very precious to us, such as a marvellous art object or a piece of jewellery. Because of this, Oriental jade dealers wear dark glasses, so that they do not give the game away when they see a particularly good example. Professional poker players also shield their eyes to conceal their pupil reactions to high cards.

Locality: Worldwide.

SHOULDER BRUSH

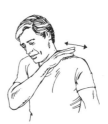

Meaning: Favour.

Action: The hand lightly brushes the gesturer's shoulder, as if removing dust.

Background: This gesture is known as 'Apple Polishing' or 'Cepillar' and indicates that someone is toadying to a dominant figure in order to gain favour.

Locality: South America.

SHOULDER PAT

Meaning: Well done me!

Action: The gesturer pats himself on the back.

Background: A joking form of self-congratulation.

Locality: Western world.

SHOULDER STRIKE

Meaning: Greeting.

Action: When two people meet they playfully strike one another on the shoulder.

Background: In the frozen north, ordinary contact gestures make little impact through the heavy clothing. The result is this more robust form of greeting.

Locality: Eskimo communities.

SHOULDERS CLASP

Meaning: Respectful greeting.

Action: The gesturer clasps his shoulders with his own hands, folding his arms across his chest in the process.

Background: In a culture where contact with another person is inhibited, the greeting ritual takes the form of hugging oneself instead of the other person. The gesturer says, in effect, 'I offer you this hug' but does so while keeping his distance.

Locality: Malaysia.

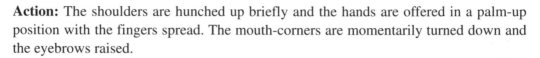

SHOULDERS SHRUG

Meaning: I do not know.

Action: The shoulders are hunched up briefly and the hands are offered in a palm-up position with the fingers spread. The mouth-corners are momentarily turned down and the eyebrows raised.

Background: The shrug is nearly always an expression of ignorance – 'I can't say', 'I can't help you', 'I have no idea' – and the helplessness of the gesturer is demonstrated by a momentary defensiveness. This is expressed in the body-hunching, as though there is some physical threat present.

Locality: Worldwide, but less common in the Far East.

SMOKE BLOW

Meaning: Sexual invitation.

Action: A man blows smoke from his cigarette into a woman's face.

Background: In most countries this action would be considered extremely offensive, but in certain regions it is an accepted gesture indicating that the man desires the woman sexually.

Locality: Northern Syria.

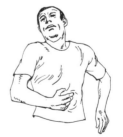

STOMACH CLASP

Meaning: I am hungry.

Action: The hand clasps the stomach.

Background: This hunger signal, suggesting the pains of an empty belly, is an alternative to the Belly Rub.

Locality: Worldwide.

STOMACH 'SAW'

Meaning: I am hungry.

Action: The edge of the hand 'saws' back and forth on the stomach.

Background: This is a local variant of the more common Stomach Clasp, signifying hunger.

Locality: Greece.

STOMACH 'STAB'

Meaning: I should kill myself!

Action: The hand mimes the act of thrusting a sword into the front of the body.

Background: This is the Japanese version of the familiar 'shooting-oneself-in-the-temple' mime of the Western world. It is based on the ancient method of committing ritual suicide in Japan called 'hari kari'. When the Japanese are acutely embarrassed, this gesture is used to indicate that 'I wish I was dead'.

Locality: Japan.

TEETH FLICK (I)

Meaning: Angry threat.

Action: The thumbnail is placed behind the upper teeth and then flicked violently forward, making a clicking noise. In a less intense version, the gesturer goes through the motion without bothering to make contact with the teeth.

Background: This is an ancient gesture made famous by Shakespeare in *Romeo and Juliet*. There it is called 'biting the thumb' and is employed as a taunt in an attempt to pick a quarrel. It was popular as an insult throughout Europe in earlier centuries and in France was given a specific name, 'La Nique', referring to the sound made by the nail clicking on the teeth. Today its geographical range has shrunk and it is unknown in northern Europe.

Locality: Today it is common in Greece and Sicily, and is still used occasionally as a threat in countries all around the Mediterranean, but seems to be on the wane.

TEETH FLICK (2)

Meaning: I have nothing.

Action: (As above, but without the expression of intense anger)

Background: The gesture is used to send two forms of negative: the mildly hostile 'I will give you nothing' to the blunt statement of fact that 'I have nothing to give'. In Arab countries there is one dominant meaning: 'I have no money', and it is often accompanied by the phrase 'neegree-neegree'.

Locality: France, Spain, Portugal, Yugoslavia, Turkey, Sardinia and in Arab cultures in both north Africa and the Middle East.

TEETH RUB

Meaning: I have nothing.

Action: The thumbnail is rubbed sideways across the teeth.

Background: This appears to be a local variant of the Teeth Flick (2) gesture.

Locality: Eastern Europe.

TEMPLE CIRCLE (1)

Meaning: Crazy!

Action: The forefinger is rotated to trace a small circle close to the temple. The movement may be in either a clockwise or an anti-clockwise direction.

Background: The gesture symbolizes the idea that the brain is rolling round and round, out of control, inside the skull.

Locality: Widespread. In most regions the direction of the rotation is of no significance, but see below.

TEMPLE CIRCLE (2)

Meaning: Crazy!

Action: As above, but the forefinger must move in an anti-clockwise direction.

Background: Here the symbolism refers to the perversity of winding in an anti-clockwise direction. A perverse or eccentric person is referred to in Japanese as 'Hidari-maki', which means literally: 'to wind counterclockwise'.

Locality: Japan.

TEMPLE CIRCLE (3)

Meaning: Vain.

Action: As above, but with the finger rotating in a clockwise direction.

Background: Purists argue that the Japanese make this subtle distinction between the clockwise and anti-clockwise versions of the gesture, but this is no longer always the case. In modern Japan, perhaps because of foreign influence, this old tradition is being eroded. Today the Temple Circle can sometimes mean 'Crazy!', regardless of the direction of the forefinger.

Locality: Japan.

TEMPLE SCREW (I)

Meaning: Crazy!

Action: The forefinger is screwed into the temple as if trying to tighten up a 'loose screw'.

Background: This gesture is related to the saying 'He has a screw loose'.

Locality: Widespread in the Western world.

TEMPLE SCREW (2)

Meaning: Crazy!

Action: The thumb and forefinger are twisted against the temple as if trying to tighten up a wing-nut.

Background: As with the previous gesture, the action symbolically tightens up the brain-casing to improve the functioning of the brain.

Locality: Southern Italy.

TEMPLE 'SHOOT'

Meaning: I should kill myself!

Action: The gesturer mimes the action of shooting himself in the temple with a handgun.

Background: When someone commits a 'faux pas' or 'puts his foot in it' at a social gathering, he may express his self-disgust by pretending to shoot himself.

Locality: Widespread in the Western world.

TEMPLE TAP (1)

Meaning: Crazy!

Action: The forefinger taps the temple several times.

Background: The Temple Tap gesture implies that the brain requires attention. The tapping action is similar to the one used to test a clock or watch that has stopped working. Unlike the Temple Circle, which can only mean 'crazy', this gesture is slightly ambiguous, as it is also used to indicate that someone is very brainy.

Locality: Widespread.

TEMPLE TAP (2)

Meaning: Clever.

Action: The finger taps the temple several times.

Background: The finger points at the brain, implying that it is working well. The message is either 'I know what's going on, I have figured it out', or 'He is very clever.'

Locality: Widespread.

TEMPLE TOUCH

Meaning: I have an idea!

Action: The forefinger touches the temple and then 'pops' off it with a forward movement.

Background: This is a variant of the 'clever' Temple Tap. It signals, not that someone else is clever, but that the gesturer himself has just had a bright idea. The finger goes to the temple to indicate cleverness, but instead of tapping the surface, it 'bounces' off it, ending up with the raised forefinger 'eureka' position.

Locality: Europe, especially France.

TEMPLES ANTLERS

Meaning: Sexual insult.

Action: With thumbs touching temples, the spread fingers are waggled at the victim.

Background: This is a variation of the horn-sign, with the antlers of a stag replacing the horns of a bull. In both cases the insulting message is that the victim is a cuckold – that his wife is unfaithful to him.

Locality: Syria.

TEMPLES EARS

Meaning: You are an ass!

Action: With the thumbs touching the temples, the fingers are fanned out sideways.

Background: A joking insult, related to the Ears Thumb gesture, it is mostly used by children. The message of this gesture is 'you have big ears like this – you are a stupid donkey, a jackass!' It is easily confused with the Temple Antlers gesture, a much more serious insult that signifies cuckoldry.

Locality: Italy.

TEMPLES HORNS

Meaning: Sexual insult.

Action: The vertical forefingers are placed against the temples, suggesting the horns of a bull.

Background: This is another variation of the insulting cuckold sign.

Locality: Widespread.

THIGH SLAP (1)

Meaning: Impatience.

Action: While standing, the hand slaps the outside of the thigh repeatedly and rhythmically.

Background: In this gesture the hand is making stylized 'locomotion' movements, suggesting the person in question wishes to depart but cannot do so for some reason. The action carries the same message as the Fingers Strum and the Foot Tap.

Locality: Widespread.

THIGH SLAP (2)

Meaning: Obscenity.

Action: The hand slaps the inside of the thigh.

Background: Because of the proximity of the genitals, slapping this part of the body is considered a highly suggestive action.

Locality: Argentina.

THIRD-FINGER POINT

Meaning: Married.

Action: The forefinger of one hand points towards the base of the third finger of the other hand.

Background: This is a gesture used to inform a friend that someone is married. The finger points at the place where the wedding ring is worn on the 'ring finger'. In some countries the ring finger is on the left hand, but in others it is on the right.

Locality: North and South America.

THROAT 'CUT' (1)

Meaning: Threat.

Action: The stiff forefinger is drawn like a knife across the throat. The action is often accompanied by the mouthing of a tearing noise, as if the 'knife' is noisily slashing the flesh.

Background: As with many mimed gestures, the performer does to himself what he would like to do to someone else.

Locality: Widespread.

THROAT 'CUT' (2)

Meaning: It is over!

Action: The stiff hand, palm down, is drawn across the throat sideways.

Background: This gesture also mimes the act of cutting someone's throat, but the message here is 'you are about to be cut off.' In other words, whatever you are doing must end right now. The action originated in television studios, when the performer had run out of time, and had to be stopped immediately. Since then it has spread to a more general usage in social situations.

Locality: Western countries.

THROAT 'CUT' (3)

Meaning: I could cut my own throat.

Action: The forefinger is drawn across the throat.

Background: When someone commits a social gaffe or 'faux pas', he may mime the act of cutting his own throat as a way of admitting his own stupidity.

Locality: Widespread.

THROAT GRASP (1)

Meaning: I will strangle you.

Action: The gesturer grasps his own throat.

Background: The action is a simple mime of what the gesturer wishes to do to another person.

Locality: Arab cultures.

THROAT GRASP (2)

Meaning: Suicide.

Action: (As above)

Background: The gesturer mimes the act of hanging himself, implying that he, or someone else, is suicidal, or that somebody else has just committed suicide.

Locality: New Guinea.

THROAT GRASP (3)

Meaning: I have had enough.

Action: (As above)

Background: This version of the gesture signals that 'I am fed up to here'.

Locality: Italy.

THROAT GRASP (4)

Meaning: Imprisonment.

Action: (As above)

Background: Used as a sign that someone has been caught and may go to jail, or a comment that someone is already in jail, or a warning that what is being done could lead to imprisonment.

Locality: South America.

THROAT GRASP (5)

Meaning: I performed badly.

Action: (As above)

Background: Used in sport to indicate that a competitor 'choked up', or tensed up, and therefore did not perform properly.

Locality: North America.

THROAT GRASP (6)

Meaning: I cannot breathe.

Action: (As above)

Background: When someone is genuinely choking on a piece of food, or some other object lodged in the throat they cannot speak clearly enough to summon help. The American Red Cross have suggested that the 'throat grasp' gesture should be given in such cases as an emergency signal. The problem for the victim is that, with so many other meanings to this particular gesture, onlookers may not be sure about the precise message being transmitted.

Locality: North America.

THROAT PINCH

Meaning: Thin.

Action: The Adam's apple is held between the thumb and forefinger.

Background: The gesture suggests a scrawny neck.

Locality: Southern Italy.

THROAT SAW

Meaning: I am fed up to here.

Action: The hand saws back and forth across the front of the neck.

Background: This is a local variant of the more familiar Chin Tap or Throat Grasp (3). Its original message was that 'I am full up with food, right up to here.' But it is now used in a more general way to say that 'I am fed up with' whatever is being discussed.

Locality: Austria.

THROAT STROKE

Meaning: I do not believe you.

Action: The forefinger moves lightly up and down the throat several times. The mouth may be opened.

Background: The gesture draws attention to the source of the words that the companion is uttering and which simply cannot be true.

Locality: South America.

THUMB ARC

Meaning: Drink.

Action: The thumb is jerked in a curved arc several times in the direction of the open mouth. The head is tipped back a little and the mouth opened.

Background: This version of the 'I am thirsty' or 'Let's have a drink' gesture mimes the action of drinking from a flask.

Locality: Spain, southern France, Italy, Iran and Arab cultures.

THUMB BACK

Meaning: In the past.

Action: The thumb is jerked backwards several times over the shoulder.

Background: This is a method of referring to the past (usually yesterday) by indicating the space behind the gesturer. It is the opposite of the 'future' gesture, the Forefinger Hop, that indicates 'tomorrow' by making a looping movement to the front of the body.

Locality: South America.

THUMB BITE

Meaning: Flirtation.

Action: The thumb is placed sideways between the teeth and bitten. It is then removed and shaken.

Background: This gesture is used by a boy when flirting with a girl. The self-inflicted pain symbolizes the agony the girl is causing the boy by withholding her charms. Its symbolism is similar to the 'fingers cool' gesture of Europe in which the hand of the boy mimes the act of cooling the hand after it has touched an imaginary hot surface.

Locality: Syria.

THUMB BLOW

Meaning: Defiance.

Action: The thumb is pushed into the pursed lips, the mouth is filled with air from the lungs and the cheeks are puffed out fully.

Background: The expression associated with this gesture is 'I don't give a damn!'

Locality: Holland.

THUMB CIRCLE

Meaning: Sexual obscenity.

Action: The erect thumb is moved in a circle.

Background: The movements of the thumb suggest the rhythmic actions of copulation.

Locality: Saudi Arabia.

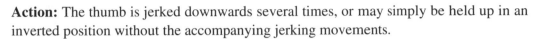

THUMB DOWN

Meaning: No good.

Action: The thumb is jerked downwards several times, or may simply be held up in an inverted position without the accompanying jerking movements.

Background: This is the antithesis of the Thumb Up gesture that signifies all is well. It originated from the ancient Rome habit of miming the stabbing of a defeated gladiator in the arena. If the crowd wanted the man to die, they thrust their thumbs downwards, as if plunging a sword into his body. Because they were seated high above the arena, this inevitably meant that the mimed stabbing movement was directed downwards, and this gave rise to the Thumb Down gesture for anything negative.

Locality: Widespread.

THUMB HITCH

Meaning: Please give me a ride.

Action: The erect thumb is swept in a curving movement in the desired direction.

Background: This is a comparatively modern gesture employed by roadside hitchhikers. Unfortunately, in certain countries (such as Sardinia, Greece, Turkey and parts of the Middle East, Africa and Australia) it has a much older meaning, with which it is sometimes confused. In those regions, the display of the erect thumb is a powerful sexual insult and it is essential for visiting hitchhikers to beg a ride with a waved, flat hand, rather than a jerked thumb.

Locality: Originally from the United States, but has since spread widely.

THUMB JERK

Meaning: Sexual insult.

Action: The stiff thumb is jerked upwards several times.

Background: The thumb here symbolizes the erect penis. Because of the close similarity between this gesture, the friendly Thumbs Up and the hitchhiker's Thumb

Hitch, misunderstandings can arise between foreign tourists and local populations. If hitchhikers at the side of a road, in certain countries, jerk their thumbs at passing cars, this is taken as a deliberate obscenity and may lead to heated exchanges rather than a free ride. In those countries where the insulting thumb gesture is popular, local hitchhikers always employ a flat hand rather than a jerked thumb. Not surprisingly, the thumb jerk is rare in North America and Europe, where the other two gestures are so well known, and they, in turn, are rare where the Thumb Jerk is commonly used as an insult. The exception to this rule is Australia, where both are employed, and where some confusion does exist.

Locality: Sardinia, Greece, Turkey, Iran, the Middle East, Russia and parts of Africa and Australia. (In Turkey it is used more specifically as a homosexual invitation signal.)

THUMB POINT

Meaning: Contempt.

Action: The thumb is pointed sideways in the direction of the victim.

Background: Jabbing the thumb in the direction of someone who is being mentioned in conversation is a deliberately insulting action. The thumb, as the 'power' digit, gives the action an aggressive threatening flavour.

Locality: Widespread.

THUMB SUCK

Meaning: He is lying.

Action: The tip of the thumb is placed between the lips, as if to suck it.

Background: This is the gesture given when someone is thought to be inventing a story.

Locality: Holland.

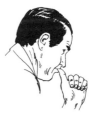

THUMB UP (1)

Meaning: O.K.

Action: The erect thumb is displayed towards a companion.

Background: This gesture has a strange origin, based on a misunderstanding. In the ancient Roman Colosseum, when the crowd wanted a vanquished gladiator to be spared, because he had fought well, they covered up their thumbs (*pollice compresso* – thumb compressed). When they wanted him killed, because he had fought badly, they mimed the action of plunging in the sword by extending their thumbs and imitating the thrusting action (*pollice verso* – thumb turned). Through mistranslation or ignorance, this opposing pair of gestures eventually changed from 'thumb cover up' to 'thumb up' for 'something good', and from 'thumb thrust' to 'thumb down' for 'something bad'. And this is the form in which we use them today.

Locality: Widespread.

THUMB UP (2)

Meaning: Male companion.

Action: (As above)

Background: Because it is thick, the thumb here symbolizes the male, contrasting with the slender little finger, which is female. In this version of the gesture, the action of showing a thumb is used to refer to any male companion, regardless of whether he is a boy friend, husband, patron or boss.

Locality: Japan.

THUMB UP (3)

Meaning: Long live the Basques!

Action: (As above)

Background: Certain gestures, such as the Victory-V, the Zeig-heil and the Communist fist, develop strong political ties that give them a powerful meaning. In Spain, this has also happened to the Thumb Up gesture, although the Spanish usage of it is not widely known elsewhere. There, it has become the emblem of the Basque Separatist Movement and visitors employing a cheerful Thumbs Up to mean 'Everything is fine!' may find themselves in serious trouble without understanding why.

Locality: North-west Spain.

THUMB UP (4)

Meaning: Nothing doing!

Action: (As above)

Background: This reported, local usage for the Thumb Up gesture requires verification. If valid, it is presumably based on the moment when a returning figure holds up an empty fist – a fist in which the thumb grips 'nothing'.

Locality: Western Punjab.

THUMB UP (5)

Meaning: Five.

Action: (As above)

Background: Because the Japanese do not use the Western Thumb Up gesture for OK, they are liable to misinterpret it, thinking that the action signifies the number five. This is because, when counting on their fingers, this is the number that is signalled by an erect thumb.

Locality: Japan.

THUMB-AND-FOREFINGER ROTATE

Meaning: Nothing doing.

Action: With the thumb and forefinger extended, the hand is rotated back and forth at the wrist.

Locality: Italy.

THUMB-AND-LITTLE-FINGER ARC

Meaning: Drink.

Action: With the thumb and little finger extended and the other fingers curled, the hand makes arcing movements towards the mouth. During this action, the thumb-tip is aimed directly at the lips.

Background: This is a gesture that mimes the act of drinking from a leather bottle by squirting a jet of liquid into the open mouth (as seen in Spain and in Arab countries). It differs from Hand 'Drink' gestures in other regions, where the mime is nearly always that of raising an imaginary glass to the lips. The message of this gesture is either 'I am thirsty' or 'Would you like a drink?'

Locality: Spain and Spanish-speaking South America. Also Arab cultures.

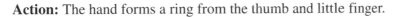

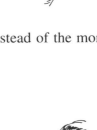

THUMB-AND-LITTLE-FINGER RING

Meaning: I got nothing.

Action: The hand forms a ring from the thumb and little finger.

Background: Here, by making the ring-sign with the little finger instead of the more usual forefinger, the gesturer signals a negative instead of a positive.

Locality: Sicily.

THUMB-AND-LITTLE-FINGER ROTATE

Meaning: Drunk.

Action: As for the Thumb-and-Little-Finger Arc, but instead of moving towards the mouth, the hand is rotated back and forth.

Background: The symbolism of the gesture is based on the idea that the drinker can no longer keep the bottle steady.

Locality: South America.

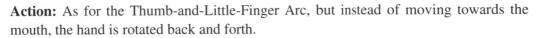

THUMB-AND-LITTLE-FINGER WAGGLE

Meaning: Friendly greeting.

Action: The arm is raised as if giving a wave. Then, with the thumb and little finger extended, and the other fingers curled, the hand is waggled gently in the air.

Background: This is a modified form of a Spanish drinking gesture. In the original version, the thumb is pointed towards the mouth, mimicking the action of drinking from a leather bottle. Here, however, the hand is raised in the air, away from the mouth. It has an interesting history. When Spanish sailors, or immigrants from the Spanish colonies of Central or South America, first arrived in the Hawaiian Islands, they made friendly gestures to the inhabitants which took the form of an invitation to join them in a drink. Their drinking gesture eventually became the general greeting signal for the islands and, in the process, lost its oral orientation. Today, most of the islanders are unaware of its Spanish origins. It is now popularly known as the 'Hang loose' or 'Aloha' gesture. Some inhabitants of the island today also call it the 'shaka' gesture, because of its repeated use by a local television comedian called 'Lucky Luck' whose catchphrase was 'it's a shaka' (= 'it's a shocker').

Locality: Hawaiian Islands.

THUMB, FOREFINGER AND LITTLE-FINGER RAISE

Meaning: I love you.

Action: The hand is raised with the thumb, forefinger and little finger all spread. The other two digits are bent down.

Background: This is a gesture borrowed from the official American Sign Language, but now employed in a wide range of social contexts by people who wish to express their love for their audiences. Sports stars, rock stars, politicians and even religious leaders have been observed to offer this sign to their followers in recent years.

Locality: Originally United States, but now spreading.

THUMB, FOREFINGER AND MIDDLE-FINGER THRUST

Meaning: Threat.

Action: The three digits are joined together and then moved rapidly forwards.

Background: The action mimes the thrust of a dagger into the enemy's body.

Locality: Saudi Arabia and Jordan.

THUMBNAIL APPLAUSE

Meaning: Sarcastic applause.

Action: The thumbnails are tapped together repeatedly, mimicking hand-clapping.

Background: This is a derisive form of applause. It is employed as a deliberate insult at the moment when true applause would be the expected result.

Locality: Holland, Spain and South America.

THUMBNAIL KISS

Meaning: I swear!

Action: The thumbnail is kissed. At the moment this is done, the forefinger rests against the thumb, but then the hand is quickly moved away from the lips and the forefinger is simultaneously shifted down to the middle of the thumb. As a result of this action, the thumb and forefinger now form a cross.

Background: A common method of swearing an oath in Catholic countries, this is the gestural equivalent of kissing a crucifix. It is sometimes accompanied by the words 'Por esta, la cruz – Te lo juro' (By this, the cross, I swear it).

Locality: Spain, South America and Central America.

THUMBNAIL PRESS

Meaning: You are a louse.

Action: The thumbnails are pressed together, as if killing a bug.

Background: This is similar to the sardonic Thumbnail Applause, but without the repeated tapping of the thumbnails against one another. Instead the nails are held together and twisted slightly.

Locality: Spain.

THUMBS BITE

Meaning: I surrender.

Action: The ends of the thumbs are placed in the mouth and the spread fingers are pointed at the onlooker.

Background: This is a local version of the more usual Arms Raise (1) 'hands up' signal of surrender.

Locality: Bedouin tribes.

THUMBS TWIDDLE

Meaning: Boredom.

Action: The fingers are interlocked and the thumbs are then rotated around one another.

Background: 'Twiddling the thumbs' is a phrase that has become synonymous with the state of boredom. It involves a mild frustration, caused by the boredom and the gesture is akin to the pacing up and down of a caged animal. It is as though, when nothing is happening, any small action is better than sitting completely still.

Locality: Widespread.

THUMBS WAGGLE

Meaning: Homosexual.

Action: The palm of one hand is placed on the back of the other and the thumbs are waggled like the wings of a bird. The fingers may be slightly interlocked.

Background: Birdlike gestures are often used to imply effeminacy in a male. In South America this gesture is called 'Pajaro', or 'The Bird'.

Locality: South America and the Middle East.

TIE SHAKE

Meaning: You can't fool me.

Action: The gesturer holds his tie up and shakes it at his companion.

Background: The gesture is used as a joking taunt, saying 'you have not caught me.'

Locality: Southern Italy.

TOE CROSS

Meaning: I swear never to return.

Action: The toe is pointed at the ground and makes the sign of the cross there.

Background: Another version of Christian oath-swearing by forming the sacred sign of the cross, this time by moving the foot on the ground. This form of the gesture is used when people wish to 'protect' themselves from a place where they have suffered misfortune and to which they pray they will never have to return.

Locality: Southern Italy.

TONGUE MULTI-PROTRUDE (1)

Meaning: Sexual invitation.

Action: The tongue is moved rapidly in and out of the mouth.

Locality: Europe and the Americas.

TONGUE MULTI-PROTRUDE (2)

Meaning: You are a liar.

Action: (As above)

Locality: Saudi Arabia.

TONGUE PROTRUDE (1)

Meaning: Insult.

Action: The tongue is protruded.

Background: This 'rude gesture' is understood all over the world because it originates in childhood. The tongue is protruded every time an infant wants to reject food that is being offered to it. From this beginning, it develops into a basic rejection signal and develops gradually from an 'I don't want it' gesture into an 'I don't want *you*' one. This then easily grows into a generally insulting signal.

Locality: Worldwide.

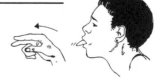

TONGUE PROTRUDE (2)

Meaning: Insult.

Action: After sticking out the tongue the gesturer makes a throwing-away movement with the right hand.

Background: In this elaboration of the gesture there is a double rejection, first with the tongue and then with the hand.

Locality: East Africa.

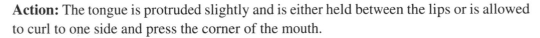

TONGUE PROTRUDE (3)

Meaning: I am concentrating hard.

Action: The tongue is protruded slightly and is either held between the lips or is allowed to curl to one side and press the corner of the mouth.

Background: This is an unconscious gesture shown by people who are fixating on a difficult manual task – such as drawing a sketch or assembling a small piece of apparatus. It again relates back to the infantile rejection reaction, only in this case there is no direct insult. The tongue is not aimed at anyone in particular and the gesturer is not even aware that it is being done. What the action is unconsciously saying is 'Please leave me in peace while I try to deal with this task'.

Locality: Worldwide.

TONGUE RUB

Meaning: Sexual obscenity.

Action: The thumb is rubbed down the tongue and the hand is lowered to the waist. In that position, with the fingers bent, the hand makes several jerking movements forward and backward.

Background: The thumb is moistened by the tongue in preparation for a mimed sexual movement by the hand.

Locality: Lebanon.

224

TONGUE TOUCH (1)

Meaning: Gossip.

Action: The bent forefinger touches the protruded tongue.

Background: The gesture draws attention to an over-active tongue.

Locality: South America.

TONGUE TOUCH (2)

Meaning: Please hurry.

Action: The tongue is touched by the tip of the forefinger, which is then placed on the tip of the nose.

Locality: Saudi Arabia.

TONGUE WAGGLE

Meaning: Sexual proposition.

Action: The tip of the tongue is wagged from side to side of the partly opened lips.

Background: The tongue anticipates the licking actions that occur during the more advanced intimacies of sexual contact.

Locality: Widespread.

TONGUE-TIP SHOW

Meaning: I didn't mean it!

Action: The tip of the tongue is protruded and then immediately withdrawn.

Background: This version of tongue protrusion is observed when someone is embarrassed at having spoken out of turn.

Locality: Tibet and southern China.

TROUSER LIFT

Meaning: Disbelief.

Action: One trouser leg is lifted fastidiously.

Background: The gesturer pretends to be sinking into deep manure, implying that the statement he has just heard is 'bullshit'. It is typically employed between males in a joking context.

Locality: United States.

WAIST BOW

Meaning: Respect.

Action: The body bends forward from the waist, with the head and eyes lowered.

Background: Bowing is an ancient form of subordinate body-lowering. Like most submissive gestures it reduces the size of the performer in relation to the onlooker. In earlier centuries, bowing was a common greeting in the West, but it is now generally reserved for formal occasions. In court circles today there is a gender distinction, with men bowing and women curtseying, but in the theatre it is usual for both actors and actresses to perform the bow at the end of a performance. In Japan bowing remains as the normal greeting gesture for use in everyday life. There the depth of the bow is carefully adjusted to the status of the bower relative to the onlooker. Seniors bow very slightly forward; subordinates bow deeply. For a western visitor to bow deeply to a person of lower status is considered bad manners, even though the intention is to be courteous in the local style.

Locality: Worldwide. Common in Asia. Infrequent in Europe, except in Germany. Rare in the United States.

WAIST OUTLINE

Meaning: She is sexy.

Action: The hands describe the curvaceous outline of a female body.

Background: This is a popular signal from one male to another about a female who has just been spotted or whose attributes are being discussed.

Locality: Europe and North America.

WRIST FLAP

Meaning: He is effeminate.

Action: The hand is flapped limply up and down in the air.

Background: This is a common insult implying effeminacy in a male. It used to be thought that it owed its meaning simply to the miming of the weaker female wrist action, but it has a more specific origin. In earlier centuries, when female costumes with very tight sleeves were popular, it was difficult for women to move their arms freely and they could only gesticulate with ease from the wrist. In this way, the flapping wrist became associated with the female gender.

Locality: Most Western countries.

WRIST GRASP

Meaning: Sexual suggestion.

Action: The gesturer's wrist is grasped with his other hand and pumped up and down.

Background: This is an obscene gesture that mimics the pelvic thrusting of copulation.

Locality: Middle East.

WRIST ROTATE

Meaning: Thief!

Action: The hand is held near the side of the body where it mimics the action of a pick-pocket scooping something from a victim's pocket.

Background: Its message is that someone is a thief or that a theft has occurred.

Locality: Holland.

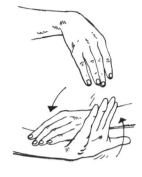

WRIST SLAP

Meaning: He is homosexual.

Action: The limp wrist is slapped from above, 'provoking' the hand to flap feebly up and down.

Background: This gesture acts out the limp-wrist caricature of the homosexual and is employed either descriptively, to indicate that a particular person is a male homosexual, or as an insult implying effeminacy.

Locality: Holland.

WRISTS CROSS (1)

Meaning: I am your prisoner.

Action: The wrists are crossed over one another as if tied together or handcuffed.

Background: The gesture is usually employed jokingly to suggest 'I am your slave', 'I give up', 'I should be arrested', or 'You can do what you like with me'.

Locality: Southern Italy.

WRISTS CROSS (2)

Meaning: He is not straight.

Action: The hands are crossed at the wrists, with the palms showing and the fingers slightly curled. This position is maintained by hooking the little fingers together. While in this posture, the hands are moved sideways.

Background: The hands imitate the shape of a crab, the suggestion being that someone moves crabwise in unexpected directions, does not keep to the 'straight and narrow', and is therefore not to be trusted.

Locality: Southern Italy.

BIBLIOGRAPHY

Andrea, P. and H.P. de Boer. 1979. *Nederlands Gebarenboekje*. Elsevier Manteau, Amsterdam. p.1-160.

Andrea, P. and H.P. de Boer. 1982. *Nieuw Nederlands Gebarenboekje*. Manteau, Amsterdam. p.1-151.

Argyle, M. 1988. *Bodily Communication*. Methuen, London. p.1-363.

Axtell, R.E. 1991. *Gestures: The Do's and Taboos of Body Language Around the World*. Wiley, New York. p.1-227.

Barakat, R.A. 1973. *'Arabic Gestures'*. Journ. Popular Culture. p.749-787.

Bauml, B.J. and F.H. Bauml. 1975. *A Dictionary of Gestures*. Scarecrow Press, Metuchen, New Jersey. p.1-249.

Bremmer, J. and H. Roodenburg. 1991. *A Cultural History of Gesture*. Polity Press, Cambridge. p.1-268.

Brun, T. 1969. *The International Dictionary of Sign Language*. Wolfe, London. p.1-127.

Bull, P. 1987. *Posture and Gesture*. Pergamon Press, Oxford. p.1-194.

Bulwer, J. 1644. *Chirologia; or the Naturall Language of the Hand*. London. p.1-191.

Bulwer, J. 1644. *Chironomia; or the Art of Manuall Rhetorique*. London. p.1-147.

Bulwer, J. 1648. *Philocophus; or the Deafe and Dumbe Mans Friend*. London. p.1-191.

Bulwer, J. 1654. *A View of the People of the Whole World*. London. p.1-590.

Calbris, G. 1990. *The Semiotics of French Gesture*. Bloomington.

Calbris, G. and J. Montredon. 1986. *Des Gestes et des Mots pour le Dire*. Paris.

Collett, P. 1993. *Foreign Bodies: A Guide to European Mannerisms*. Simon and Schuster, London. p.1-215.

Critchley, M. 1939. *The Language of Gesture*. Arnold, London. p.1-128.

Critchley, M. 1975. *Silent Language*. Butterworths, London. p.1-231.

D'Angelo, L. 1969. *How to be an Italian*. Price, Stern, Sloane, Los Angeles. p.1-93.

Darwin, C. 1872. *The Expression of Emotions in Man and Animals*. John Murray, London. p.1-374.

Davis, F. 1973. *Inside Intuition: What We Know About Nonverbal Communication.* McGraw-Hill, New York. p.1-236.

De Jorio, A. 1832. *La Mimica degli Antichi Investigata nel Gestire Napoletano.* Naples. p.1-357.

Efron, D. 1972. *Gesture, Race and Culture.* Mouton, The Hague. p.1-226.

Eibl-Eibesfeldt, I. 1989. *Ethology: The Biology of Behaviour.* Holt, Rinehart and Winston, New York. p.1-848.

Fast, J. 1970. *Body Language.* Evans, New York. p.1-192.

Fast, J. 1977. *The Body Language of Sex, Power and Aggression.* Jove, New York. p.1-190.

Green, J.R. 1968. *Gesture Inventory for the Teaching of Spanish.* Chilton Books, Philadelphia.

Guthrie, R.D. 1976. *Body Hot Spots.* Van Nostrand Reinhold, New York. p.1-240.

Lamb, W. 1965. *Posture and Gesture.* Duckworth, London. p.1-189.

Lamb, W. and E. Watson. 1979. *Body Code: The Meaning in Movement.* Routledge and Kegan Paul, London. p.1-190.

Leith, L. Von Der. 1967. *Dansk Dove-Tegnsprog.* Akademisk Forlag, Copenhagen. p.1-175.

Lyle, J. 1990. *Body Language.* BCA, London. p.1-144.

McNeill, D. 1992. *Hand and Mind: What Gestures Reveal About Thought.* University Press, Chicago. p.1-416.

Meo-Zilo, G. and S. Mejia. 1980-1983. *Diccionario de Gestos: Espana E Hispanoamerica.* 2 vols. Bogota.

Monahan, B. 1983. *A Dictionary of Russian Gesture.* Ann Arbor.

Morris, D. 1977. *Manwatching: A Field-Guide to Human Behaviour.* Jonathan Cape, London. p.1-320.

Morris, D. 1987. *Bodywatching: A Field-Guide to the Human Species.* Jonathan Cape, London. p.1-256.

Morris, D., P. Collett, P. Marsh and M. O'Shaughnessy. 1979. *Gestures: Their Origins and Distribution.* Jonathan Cape, London. p.1-296.

Munari, B. 1963. *Supplemento al Dizionario Italiano.* Muggiani Editore, Milan. p.1-115.

Nierenberg, G.I. and H. Calero. 1971. *How to Read a Person Like a Book.* Hawthorn New York. p.1-180.

Papas, W. 1972. *Instant Greek.* Papas, Athens.

Pease, A. 1984. *Body Language.* Sheldon Press, London. p.1-152.

Ricci-Bitti, P.E. 1976. *Communication by Gesture in North and South Italians.* Italian Journal of Psychology, 3, p.117-126.

Saitz, R.L. and E.C. Cervenka. 1972. *Handbook of Gestures: Colombia and the United States.* Mouton, The Hague. p.1-164.

Seward, J. 1979. *Japanese in Action.* Weatherhill, New York. p.1-213.

Scheflen, A.E. 1972. *Body Language and the Social Order*. Prentice-Hall, New Jersey. p.1-208.

Whitby, M. 1979. *Gestos de Mano: A Comparative Study of Gestures in Ecuador and Peru*. Oxford. p.1-92.

Wildeblood, J. 1973. *The Polite World. A Guide to English Manners and Deportment*. Davis-Poynter, London. p.1-224.

Wundt, W. 1973. *The Language of Gestures*. Mouton, The Hague. p.1-149.

Wylie, L.W. 1977. *Beau Gestes: A Guide to French Body Talk*. Cambridge, Mass.